Extreme North

Extreme North

A Cultural History

BERND BRUNNER

Translated by Jefferson Chase

W. W. NORTON & COMPANY
Independent Publishers Since 1923

Originally published in the German language as "Die Erfindung des Nordens" by Bernd Brunner
Copyright © 2019 by Verlag Kiepenheuer & Witsch, Cologne/Germany
Translation copyright © 2022 by W. W. Norton & Company, Inc.

For information about permission to reproduce selections from this book, write to
Permissions, W. W. Norton & Company, Inc., 500 Fifth Avenue, New York, NY 10110

For information about special discounts for bulk purchases, please contact
W. W. Norton Special Sales at specialsales@wwnorton.com or 800-233-4830

Manufacturing by Lake Book Manufacturing
Book design by Chris Welch
Production manager: Anna Oler

ISBN 978-0-393-88100-4

W. W. Norton & Company, Inc., 500 Fifth Avenue, New York, N.Y. 10110
www.wwnorton.com

W. W. Norton & Company Ltd., 15 Carlisle Street, London W1D 3BS

1 2 3 4 5 6 7 8 9 0

The sailor cannot see the *north*
but knows the *needle* can.

—EMILY DICKINSON (1862)

Contents

Extreme North

The Northern Unicorn

To understand the North, a good starting point is the cabinet of wonders of Ole (short for Olaf) Worm (1588–1654), a professor of medi-
cine in Copenhagen, one of the founders of Scandinavian archaeology, and
a royal antiquary of the Dano-Norwegian Realm. Or to be more accurate,
the engraving of the cabinet, made by a certain G. Wingendorp in 1655,
which serves as the frontispiece of the folio *Museum Wormianum*. Printed
in Amsterdam and Leyden and written in Latin, the book serves as a catalog
of Worm's collection of curiosities, mostly from the European High North.
It documents the specimens of the collection and divides them up, chapter
by chapter, into neat categories of fossils, plants, and animals. Following
the wisdom of his time, Worm considered fossils subterranean "growths,"
with petrification produced by "a stone-forming juice"—an interpretation
that shows how different seventeenth-century scientific knowledge was
from science today.

Ole Worm's *Museum Wormianum*. Natural History Museum of Denmark

The engraving shows a single room crammed with fascinating and puzzling objects from the collection. Zoologically well-informed readers with a bit of imagination can identify at the right-hand edge a great auk, a flightless seabird. Worm claimed the creature had been sent to him from the Faroe Islands, between Scotland, Norway, and Iceland in the North Atlantic, and he kept it as a pet until he died. Among the more easily discernible objects is also a miniature polar bear hanging from the ceiling next to a kayak. On the left-hand side of the back wall, there's a pair of skis and an assortment of harpoons and arrows. Closer to the front is a bizarre object made of oddly formed bones joined at an angle underneath several sets of antlers. It's a stool made of a whale's vertebrae.

Above this curious piece of furniture and a bit further back, viewers can make out the jewel of Worm's collection: an animal skull with a long, sharp, spiral tusk protruding from the base of the forehead. It's from a narwhal, an aquatic mammal with the Latin name *Monodon monoceros* that rarely ventures from its Arctic home. Previously, people in both Europe and the Far East believed that such tusked skulls were evidence of the existence of unicorns, and in fact, Worm suggested that these mythical beasts had been inspired by real, though rare, narwhals in the northern seas. To say that the skull was worth its weight in gold would be a massive understatement. It was actually valued at ten times that amount. Narwhal tusks were considered such prized commodities that a bit later, in the seventeenth century, a new Danish royal throne was created featuring twisted legs and struts made from narwhal tusks as well as the usual gold decorations.

The engraving of Worm's cabinet also depicts a number of smaller items, such as minerals and plants carefully organized into categories and neatly sorted into boxes labeled in large Latin letters. The first minerals in the collection came from mine surveyors working in Norway, on the Faroe Islands, and in Scania, the southernmost province of Sweden. The table in the center of the room seems like a spot to sit down with specific objects and examine them more closely—although it's empty and only features the title and date of the folio cum catalog. Most of the treasures depicted in the engraving remain something of a mystery; while they all originated somewhere in the vast expanses of the "North," their exact provenance has never been clearly established.

The room doesn't seem to have been designed with comfort in mind—the whale-bone stool doesn't look very inviting to sit on. While not the only one of its kind, Worm's cabinet is a paradigm of a collection reflecting its originator's lively curiosity, his search for divine intention, and his fascination with realms unknown. Many of the artifacts in this cabinet have to do with fishing and hunting, and none—leaving aside a few pieces of Danish jewelry—are the products of what we commonly consider "artistic" endeavors. But art wouldn't become a focus of collections like this until the nineteenth century.

As a physician and polymath, Ole Worm possessed an incredible thirst for knowledge. After studying in Marburg, Padua, and Basel, Worm set out on a lengthy journey to meet a number of Europe's most prominent scientists and visit some of its most famous collections—in what is now Italy, the Netherlands, and Germany. The most famous and ambitious of these was the one that the Italian naturalist Ulisse Aldrovandi had created in Bologna—his "theater of nature," comprising some seven thousand natural objects either collected during his expeditions in Italy or acquired through his vast network of associates. Aldrovandi is said to have desperately wanted to travel to America, but when he had the opportunity at the age of 65, he felt he was too frail to do it. The collection made a lasting impact on Worm and inspired him to create his own cabinet—although with a somewhat different emphasis. Worm would make use of his many contacts in high latitudes.

An important source were Danish friends living abroad whom Worm asked to send interesting items. Visitors from Iceland likely sent him additional items. Even some of his patients supplied material. At some point, it must have become common knowledge that Worm was obsessed with objects from the High North and other places. Worm's passion had little in common with "science" as we understand it today. Collectors in his day were interested in more or less everything that was exotic, since they felt that it provided evidence of God's vast creative power.

Worm was justifiably proud of his collection, and records indicate that he gave lectures on specific pieces displayed there. By selecting and arranging his artifacts, Worm was also trying to "make it possible for my public to touch them with their own hands and see them with their own eyes." People came from far and wide to view Worm's cabinet and gain a sense of the vast expanse of the North. Even after Worm died, visitors from throughout Europe continued to travel to Copenhagen to get a look at his life's work.

Unfortunately, only about forty of the objects survive today. Over the centuries, fires destroyed large sections of the city, and the exact location of Museum Wormianum has become a mystery. But some of Worm's treasures can be found in Denmark's Museum of Natural History in Copenhagen, while others are housed in the Danish National Museum.

Beyond the Borders
of the Known World

The location "north" is very much in the eye of the beholder. Take, for example, the volcanic Bouvetøya (Bouvet Island). This almost completely ice-covered speck of Norway, just about 19 square miles in area, is uninhabited and has been a nature preserve for half a century. In 1739, French mariner Jean-Baptiste Charles Bouvet de Lozier and his companions sighted it, but the forbidding glacial cliffs prevented them from landing. Germany's legendary Valdivia expedition was more successful, spending five days in November 1898 studying the island. Britain first claimed this remote outpost, but in 1927, Norway's Harald Horntvedt explored it more thoroughly and planted the Norwegian flag there, leading Britain eventually to cede its claim. In one sense, Bouvetøya lies in the North—but only from the perspective of the South Pole. The island is located between South Africa and Antarctica and is known as "the last place on earth." Only seals, penguins, and local seabirds call it home.

As this example illustrates, the North begins where the South ends. But where does the border between them reside, and how can we recognize it? For the great German poet Johann Wolfgang von Goethe, the Brenner Pass in the Alps connecting Austria and Italy constituted the "dividing line between the South and the North." But in 1771, August Ludwig von Schlözer took up this question in his book *General Northern History*, writing: "We Germans do not consider ourselves to be part of the North; only the Frenchman views our land as his North, and he speaks of Berlin as we do of Stockholm. Spanish writers commonly understand the North as Great Britain, and it is of course natural that African geographers and historians refer to the Mediterranean as the North Sea and believe that all Europeans are northern peoples."

On the British Isles themselves, signs on the motorway commonly direct drivers to "the North" and "the South." But where does the British North begin? In Edinburgh? Or somewhere even farther up the island? The Scots used to be so wary of being lumped together with other northern European peoples that for contrast they eagerly drew attention to other, more northerly regions considered completely uncivilized. In his *Daemonologie* of 1597, Scotland's King James VI pointedly asserted "witchcraft . . . to be most common in such wild partes of the worlde, as Lap-land and Fin-land, or in our North Iles of Orknay and Schet-land." Daniel Defoe could be credited for one of the most daring dividing lines between North and South in that his was diagonal rather than straight. That was because of the route he chose for his *Tour through the Whole Island of Great Britain* (1724), with the nonhorizontal River Trent marking the border. Defoe considered hilly Lincolnshire to be in the South while putting Derbyshire and parts of Nottinghamshire in the North, despite the fact that they are all on the same latitude!

Moving over to the New World: A compass might point out that while Alaska is the northernmost US state, it is almost never referred to as part of the North—politically speaking, it aligns with the American South (Alaska and the Gulf states Texas, Louisiana, Mississippi, and Alabama overwhelmingly depend on fossil-fuel exploitation), while Hawaii, the south-

ernmost US state in terms of geography, is a reliable part of the political
North. Something similar applies to many of the contiguous US states as
well. Idaho is never called a northern state, whereas New Jersey invariably
is. The logic of the frontier and its accompanying myths and the rift of
the Civil War may not actually invalidate geographical coordinates, but
they certainly do program Americans' use and understanding of the terms
North and South.

People still view their homes as the center of the world, the norm, the
geographical heart of things, even if they live in isolated northern spots. At
the North Pole—the "absolute north," the points of the compass are meaningless. For the Danes, the North Sea isn't north of anything—they call it
the Vesterhavet, the West Sea. In Great Britain, this same body of water
was long known as the German Sea.

The concept of "North" represents a space both real and imaginary—one
that, depending on the era, might include the borders of northern and
Celtic-influenced Europe, the northern parts of the British Isles, the English
colonies of North America, and beyond. At the beginning of the nineteenth century, before the competing concepts of the "West" and "East"
became Europe's dominant paradigm, Russia was commonly considered
part of the North. "Where is the north, exactly?" Canadian author Margaret Atwood asked. Atwood spent many years of her childhood in the woods
of northern Quebec and certainly represents a touchstone of her country's
identity. "It's not only a place but also a direction, and as such its location
is relative: to the Mexicans, the United States is the north, to Americans,
Toronto is, even though it's on roughly the same latitude as Boston. Wherever it is for us, there's a lot of it."

The word "north" has Indo-Germanic roots and originally meant "left of
sunrise." Like all the directions of the compass, the north serves as a reas-
suring coordinate to orient us in space, but over time it has also become layered with cultural and political meanings, baggage even. The same is true
of the north's antithesis, the south, of course. For centuries, the Northern
Hemisphere has been far more affluent and technologically advanced than
the southern one. But here, too, the terms are freighted with economic,

political, and cultural significance. The term "Global South" is often used to indicate the world's poorer, less industrialized countries, but it is hardly geographically exact: Mexico is considered part of the Global South while Australia and New Zealand are classed with the North. China—at least for the time being—is defined as southern in this sense, while Japan belongs to the North. The relations of power between the perceived North and South have perennially led the former to be coopted for chauvinist and racist ideas in the modern era. Imperialists from the North felt entitled to colonize supposedly backward peoples from the South (as well as Indigenous populations from the North), while self-serving notions of "Nordic" superiority were an integral part of the murderous National Socialist ideology of anti-Semitism and racism.

The story of the North varies depending on the language in which it is told, the significance attached to it, and the types of yearning it evokes—often in competition with the other points of the compass and geographical horizons. Certainly, the North (first northern Europe, then North America) was explored and discovered, but it was also, from the very beginning, an invention. It is not always possible to distinguish clearly between exploration and discovery, on the one hand, and forms of mythologization and appropriation guided by specific political, economical, colonial, and ideological interests, on the other. These ideas followed their own rules of development. In fact, in many cases, the multifaceted lore of the North was spread by people who had never actually set foot there.

Left of Sunrise

The center of the world for the Europeans of antiquity, for people like Herodotus (ca. 484–ca. 425 BCE), was the extended Mediterranean. This is evident in a map of that era that depicts the Mediterranean, the Black Sea, and their environs relatively realistically, whereas the northwest of the European continent is rendered as a single curved line that offers no intimation at all of the British Isles or Scandinavia. That wasn't Herodotus's or anyone else's fault, of course. People could only depict on their maps what they knew from personal experience—or had at least read or heard about. The North was a phantasmagoric dark spot beyond the border of the Greco-Roman universe, on the other side of the Alps and the Black Sea.

The ancient Greeks invented the legendary region of Hyperborea and located it in the European northeast, beyond the north wind Borea, which was itself named after the god who brought winter. They imagined it as a land of plenty, populated by giants, wise, happy, and immortal, who devoted themselves to music and dance and knew neither illness nor other human plagues. The catch was that there was no way for mortal men and women to get there. The Greek geographer Strabo, who came much later (64 or 63 BCE–ca. 24 CE), had a far more concrete view of the North as encompassing northwestern Gaul, the British Isles, the Lower Rhineland and Scandinavia.

Where was the legendary island of Thule, which was supposedly discovered by the Greek astronomer Pytheas of Massalia in the fourth century BCE? It was said to be a six-day trip north of the British Isles, amidst a frozen sea impossible to cross either by boat or by foot. Was it possible that Pytheas made it as far as Iceland, the Faroe Islands, or even Greenland? There was a document, apparently entitled "Over the Ocean," that described Pytheas's journey, but it was only preserved in references in works of other authors and astronomers. Thule—or Ultima Thule, as it was also known—would over the course of time be identified as Iceland, the Orkney Islands, the Faroe Islands, and even Norway. The term "Thule" was often used as a synonym for the North or the Arctic, the latter of which was derived from the Greek *Arktikos*, "of the giant bear"—the constellation of Ursa Major that was so clearly visible in the northern skies. Doubts about Thule's precise location didn't prevent cartographers as late as the sixteenth century from including it on their maps. It was standard practice for them to fill in blank spaces as best they could even in the absence of exact knowledge.

From early on, it was clear that the known world (from the perspective of the Greeks and Romans) was constantly expanding. In the first century BCE, the playwright Seneca included this motif in *Medea*, where the chorus sings: "All bounds have been removed, cities have set their walls in new lands, and the world, now passable throughout, has left nothing where it once had place: the Indian drinks of the cold Arazes, the Persians quaff the Elbe and the Rhine. There will come an age in the far-off years when Ocean shall unloose the bonds of things, when the whole broad earth shall be revealed, when Tethys shall disclose new worlds and Thule not be the limit of the lands."

The chorus would be proved right, as the horizon moved increasingly farther north. Thule occurs again in the geographical summary *Liber de Mensura Orbis Terrae* by the Irish monk Dícuil around 825 BCE, and from the context we can conclude that this time it refers to Iceland. Before the ninth century, when Norwegians first settled the Faroe Islands and Iceland, the Shetland Islands were considered the northern limit of the inhabited world. The distance from there to Iceland is roughly the same as the length of northwestern England. Along with the Orkney Islands and the Hebrides, the Shetlands were a springboard to Norway on one side and Iceland and Greenland on the other.

For a long time, in Europe, the North was considered the realm of the devil, the place from whence evil would come upon the world. By contrast, the Middle East was where the religions of the Old World had developed. The prophet Jeremiah further fleshed out the dichotomy, specifying that evil would take the form of invading northern hordes. In the superstitions of many cultures, northern peoples of various stripes have been considered harbingers of doom. Most famously the barbarian hordes from the North were blamed for the fall of Rome, while scholars now believe it collapsed under the weight of its own internal conflicts. Since antiquity, the North (as well as the West) was regarded as a region of cold and darkness, devoid of sunlight and inimical to life. This convenient interpretive system remained in place throughout the Middle Ages and continued in the speculations of sixteenth- and seventeenth-century alchemy.

The twelfth-century medieval mystic Hildegard von Bingen derived her world view from Adam's turn to the east after his creation. To Adam's right was the blessed South, and to his left was the dark North (and it's probably no coincidence that "left" in contemporary Italian is *sinistro*, which is derived from the Latin *sinister*). According to Hildegard, the north was the direction from which the church was menaced, and a "threatening, angrily growling bear" was the origin of the "godless" North Wind, "divorced of any utility, felicity and holiness" and bringing only misfortune and storms. The perniciousness of the North Wind was the basis for the character of the other three winds, which blew in opposition to it. Thus, for Hildegard, the North was a monstrous place.

These vague ideas about the North became more concrete as contact, both hostile and friendly, was established with the people who lived there. Although the relatively small population of northern Europe was spread out over a vast area, they repeatedly demonstrated their iron fortitude in battle. The Romans discovered that to their detriment in the year 9 CE when they tried to extend their territory to the Elbe River and suffered a massive defeat at the hands of the Cherusci, an early Germanic people, in the Battle of the Teutoburg Forest. Another wake-up call came toward the end of that century when the Roman legions faced tens of thousands of Caledonians in Scotland. The Romans might have prevailed in the legendary Battle of Mons Graupius, in the year 83 or 84 CE, but the historian Tacitus still wrote of the great respect Rome's soldiers had for the persistence of the "barbarians." Tacitus also famously described in detail the mentality and customs of the "Germanic tribes," using such termss as *simplicitas* (simplicity), *libertas* (love of freedom), and also *pigritia* (laziness). It was Tacitus, by the way, who invented the term "Germania" for a region in which he located various ill-defined groups of people—contrary to the commonly held opinion that stipulated a coherent people. It was certainly never a term used by the Germanic tribes themselves.

During the centuries that followed, forays by aggressive Scandinavian warriors from the north left many people in the south fearing for their lives. Vikings from the Norwegian fjords carried out terrifying raids, first in England, beginning with an attack on Lindisfarne Castle in 793 CE. In 845 CE, Vikings launched a nighttime attack on Hamburg, burning down the monasteries and the library and killing those unable to flee the city. It took a long time for what was back then a small settlement to recover from being so brutally sacked. Then 150 years later, the Vikings once again sailed up the Elbe River and terrorized the city of Stade.

The commercial network of the Vikings was gigantic, stretching from the northern Atlantic to Russia, central Asia, and the Arabian Peninsula. In this sense, they were pioneers of globalization, dealing in honey, amber, dried meat, and pelts. They also sold loot from the cities they sacked. Their boats were powered by the strength of human arms and the wind. When winds were favorable, they were even able to sail their vessels against river currents, having adopted the square rig sail that had been used for centuries in the Mediterranean.

In 860 CE, the Varangians, a Swedish subgroup of the Vikings in an extended sense of the term, attacked Constantinople, and in 885 CE, Danish Vikings invaded Paris. In subsequent centuries, the Normans conquered Normandy, southern Italy, and England. The Norwegian-Icelandic seafarer Erik the Red discovered Greenland in 980 CE. Although climate historians recently discovered that temperatures were much higher than previously thought and there are green areas inside two fjord systems in the southwest, it is rather unlikely that grain or vegetables grew there. Erik named it Greenland nonetheless, presumably to make it sound more attractive to settlers. His trick worked. Before long, twenty-five ships set sail for the island from Iceland. Fourteen reached their destination. Erik's son Leif Erikson extended his voyages further west, making it to the northeastern coast of the North American continent, what is now Nova Scotia or New Brunswick. He called the area Vinland—the word "vin" meaning field or meadow in Old Norse. It is often asserted that Leif Erikson got lost, but that's not very likely. Since the 1960s, historians have speculated that the Vikings navigated with the help of the *sólarstein* (sunstone), which allowed them to determine the position of the sun when skies were overcast; the polarizing properties of minerals such as Iceland spar could help them determine the azimuth, a coordinate of the sun. Such crystals are mentioned in the late Islandic sagas of the twelfth and thirteen centuries, and they may in fact have been pieces of transparent Icelandic calcite. Most likely, the Vikings sailed close to the coasts and were thus able to navigate the relative short stretches of open sea between Iceland and Greenland and Greenland and Newfoundland.

In any case, images of wild peoples from what was regarded as the dark, barbaric fringes persisted for quite some time in Europe, yielding only after the consolidation of the Scandinavian dominions, which were connected above all by blood relations and were by no means states in the modern sense, and the twelfth-century rise of the Hanseatic league, a confederation of towns and merchant guilds extending its commercial activities from the North and Baltic Seas to southern Scandinavia and Iceland.

The Vikings weren't the only ones sailing the seas of the High North establishing connections. Irish monks are thought to have sailed to the Faroe Islands and Iceland as early as the seventh century—most likely they were looking for solitude rather than trying to convert the few heathens who had settled there. In 1136, a monastery was founded in Archangelsk in northern Russia, and one hundred years after that, monasteries dotted the map in Scandinavia and Iceland. With the increasing activity of missionaries, Christianity would also remain an important bond connecting Europe's North and South for centuries—until the Reformation and the Thirty Years' War, which would pit northern and southern Europe against one another.

The travels of the Vikings and the monks led to cultural exchanges that birthed legends, their mythic imagery mixing fact and fiction. The first author to approach the topic systematically was the eleventh-century cleric Adam of Bremen, who was able to interview not only fellow clerics in foreign monasteries, but also seamen, merchants, and even King Sven Estridsen of Denmark. Adam preserved a lot of valuable information about the "constitution of the lands in the North" as it was understood around the turn of the second millennium—including the idea of a hellish maelstrom as the sea's source, capable of dragging all the world's ships down to the watery depths, the abyss. This conceit was hardly as outlandish as it may seem, because it is—in part—based in fact. Something comparable to the mythic maelstrom did and does indeed still exist in the form of the Moskenstraumen, a system of powerful tidal eddies and whirlpools in the Lofoten archipelago between the Norwegian Sea and the Vestfjorden.

The report *De inventione fortunata* of the Oxford cleric Nicolas de Linna, who undertook a voyage to the northernmost islands of the globe around 1360, adds to the catalog of mythologized natural wonders in the

Northern Seas. Ultimately, having ostensibly arrived at the North Pole, he claimed to have seen a gigantic stone magnet surrounded by a sea of amber.

The idea of a magnetic mountain in some impossibly remote location had been around since the time of Pliny the Elder and Ptolemy. Because no such phenomenon had ever been sighted in waters above the North Cape, the famous northernmost outpost of the Scandinavian Peninsula, it was assumed that the mountain had to be even farther north. As explorers ventured ever onward, the location of this point on the compass was pushed farther and farther, to the uppermost reaches of Greenland and then to the North Pole itself. In the thirteenth century, Dante Alighieri took a different tack, discarding the idea of a mountain and proposing that magnetic forces emanated from the North Star.

Before people understood that Earth itself was the magnet, the idea of such a mountain was a welcome explanation for the fact that the needle of the compass always pointed north. That fact was cited as a reason not to voyage there. To the northwest of Norway on the curved map of the world drawn by Benedictine monk Andreas Walsperger in Konstanz in 1448, we find the warning: "This great sea cannot be passed because of the magnets." On the map made by Johann Ruysch in 1508, northern Greenland carries the legend: "Here is the beginning of the Amber Sea. The ship's compass no longer points steadily, and ships carrying iron are unable to [break free of the pull and] return."

A map produced by geographer Gerhard Mercator in 1595 gave concrete shape to this mysterious formation, depicting what he called a *Rupus Nigra et Altissima* ("Very High Black Cliff") in the open sea of the North Pole. It was bordered by four separate landmasses and surrounded by a giant whirlpool, Mercator's version, perhaps, of the maelstrom. Though the maelstrom might have seemed forbidding, the idea that the sea at the North Pole might be free of ice inspired hopes that Europeans could reach the Far East via a northeast passage. This sparked a whole series of polar expeditions, most of which ended in catastrophe because the explorers neglected to set sail in time to get back to warmer climes. (Curiously, some Dutch seafarers not only claimed to have reached the North Pole by ship but that

Even famous mapmaker Gerhard Mercator continued to believe in an open North Pole sea surrounded by ice-free water (1595). *Courtesy of Wolfgang Horner*

the temperatures there were as warm as Amsterdam in summer.) With more accurate reports of the Arctic, Mercator's map became obsolete by the 1630s, but some people continued to believe an open North Pole sea up until the nineteenth century. What started as a myth lived on for a long time as a dubious hypothesis.

So why did sixteenth-century cartographers eventually decide to put the north exclusively at the top of their maps? Why did this mode of representation become the dominant one? The practice goes all the way back to the second-century Greco-Roman mathematician and astronomer Claudius Ptolemy, if we are to believe the surviving copies of his works made by Byzantine monks more than a thousand years later, in the thirteenth century. The cartographers who created the first *mappae mundi*—Mercator, Henricus Martellus Germanus, and Martin Waldseemüller—respected Ptolemy as a leading authority, took their cues from him, and adopted his habit of putting the north at the top. Nonetheless, the Christian maps of the Middle Ages chose another perspective. A map of Europe and Africa made by Venetian seafarer and cartographer Andrea Bianco in the fifteenth century has the east on top and Jerusalem in the middle. Similarly, in maps from the Islamic world, north often appears at the bottom, as in Moroccan Muhammad al-Idrisi's *Tabula Rogeriana*, made in 1154 for King Roger II of Sicily. The same is true of the 1459 *mappa mundi* of Fra Mauro, even if it is today usually reprinted in repolarized form (it just has to be flipped on its head to make sense to us). One possible reason is that fifteenth-century compasses pointed south. While it's difficult to generalize about the sophisticated Chinese mapmaking tradition, the famous "Composite Map of the Ming Empire," possibly created at the end of the fourteenth century, has the north at the top.

With the waning of Christian or Muslim views of the world that had put the east or south at the top, the north secured its fixed spot at the top of maps. But as self-evident as that shift might seem today, there was no strictly logical reason for the change. Apart from Ptolemy's precedent, there are at least two other potential reasons why the north drifted to the top of maps. One is its use in navigation. Before the compass was imported from China via the Arab world around 1300, European seafarers used the stars to tell what direction they were headed in. The most useful one was the North Star, since it remained in one place, almost exactly at due north, while the other fixed stars seemed to move around the sky because of Earth's rotation. The compass likewise pointed north (with the exception mentioned earlier). Invented in China some two thousand years ago, during the Han dynasty, the compass was made of the naturally magnetized lodestone and used for geomancy (a method of divination that interprets markings on the ground or the patterns formed by tossed soil, rocks, or sand) and fortune-telling. By the time it came to be used for navigation on the seas, during the Song dynasty, it already had the needles we associate with the compass today.

Another plausible explanation may be that information on the upper margin of maps was more easily visible and thus made to seem more important. European mapmakers, of course, lived in the Northern Hemisphere, so they may simply have wanted to see their own homeland as occupying a privileged position in the world.

No list of geographical flights of fancy would be complete without the legendary lost city of Atlantis. Though Plato had located it in the middle of the Atlantic Ocean, seventeenth-century Swedish polymath Olof Rudbeck the Elder, the son of the bishop of Västerås, boldly moved it to his homeland, specifically to Uppsala. This was the birth of a northern Arcadia and a highly speculative, indeed evidence-free, off-the-cuff attempt to create a basis for the idea of the North's—and, in particular, Sweden's—innate superiority. The saying *"Ex septentrione lux"* (the light comes from the north) has been attributed to Rudbeck, who also strengthened the idea that Swedes were actually descended from Goths, which had been the guiding principle of Swedish historians for over a century.

Over the centuries, others followed Rudbeck and moved Atlantis farther to the north—although often to places of which the Swedish patriot would hardly have approved. One such imitator was Jean-Sylvain Bailly, the first mayor of Paris (albeit only from July to October 1789), the president of the first National Assembly, and an astronomer who had calculated the orbit of Halley's comet. Bailly was convinced that Atlantis had been located on the islands of Svalbard, Greenland, and Novaya Zemlya, before it collapsed and tumbled into the sea. He also assumed that Earth's core had formerly been warmer and the atmosphere near the poles less cloudy, so that a kind of eternal spring had predominated. As the planet cooled, he thought, the Atlantans—the descendants of an age-old culture—had been forced to migrate, possibly to the Caucasus, thought to be where Europeans had originated. Bailly carried on an argumentative correspondence with no less an intellect than Voltaire about this and other related topics.

By the time Ole Worm assembled his cabinet of wonders, the 1539 *Carta marina* of Swedish bishop Olaus Magnus was over one hundred years old. The first edition of this land and sea map of northwestern Europe, printed in Venice, consisted of nine individual sheets and depicted all manner of sea monsters, the most famous of which was a 200-foot sea serpent allegedly spotted by fishermen on the Norwegian coast: *Serpens norvegicus.* It adorned the upper portion of the middle of the map, which showed a scarlet red monstrosity wrapping itself around a sailing vessel, obviously with the intent of dragging it down to the bottom of the sea. It was the visual illustration of sailors' tales that the serpent appeared on bright summer nights. The maelstrom also put in an appearance, to the northeast of the serpent, on the same latitude as the Lofoten archipelago.

With his reports about the exotic creatures at home in the sea, Olaus Magnus had alerted would-be explorers to the possibility of perhaps dangerous encounters, no doubt occasionally inspiring them to think twice about their travel plans. The most awesome of such encounters were definitely those with whales. Most seafarers only glimpsed whales from a distance, if at all. Magnus had himself seen the real-life animals he depicted on the Scandinavian landmass during a journey there from 1518 to 1519, but for marine creatures he had to rely on sailors' descriptions. Nonetheless, compared with the map made by the humanistic theologian Jakob Ziegler only a few years before, the first one ever to depict Finland, Magnus's map was a major step forward, one that in the words of Scandinavian Studies professor Stephan Michael Schröder would "shape the view of northern Europe cartographically for almost a century and discursively for much longer." That was true despite the fact that it was full of "technical shortcomings in the drawing of the degrees of latitude," ignored the points of the compass, depicted places in the wrong location, divided Greenland in two, and made "Finland much too pointed" and "northern Scandinavia, Iceland and the Faroe Islands much too large."

Magnus combined geographical, military, ethnographic, and biological

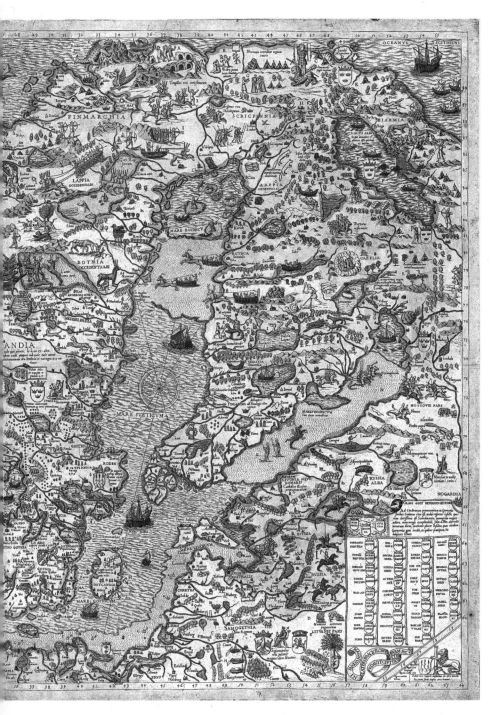

Olaus Magnus's *Carta marina* shows a multitude of fantastic sea monsters.

Courtesy of Wolfgang Horner

observations about plants and animals, which he supplemented with narratives and legends that often crossed the line into fantasy. The map we have just described was accompanied by his twenty-two-volume *Historia de gentibus septentrionalibus* (description of the northern peoples), first published in 1555. This work, richly illustrated with woodcuts, had an immediate effect and was quickly translated from Latin into Italian and German, then French, Spanish, English, and Dutch. Magnus composed it in exile in Rome, where he had fled after refusing to endorse the Swedish king's adoption of the Reformation. The Vatican financed and was the first to publish Magnus's *Historia* as way of not giving up on Catholicism in Sweden. Magnus's work did not succeed in bringing Sweden back into the Catholic fold, but it did unleash a number of similar reports about the countries of northern Europe that often quoted liberally from it.

A 1558 pamphlet titled "On the Discovery of Frisland, Iceland, Greenland and Estotiland" purported to document a voyage made by the Venetian Zeno brothers to northern waters 160 years earlier, in the late fourteenth century. In it, Nicolò Zeno the Elder describes undertaking a journey to England and Flanders only to be blown off course with his crew and wreck his ship off the coast of Frisland—an island in the northern Atlantic that was supposedly larger than Ireland and that we today know was entirely fictional. There Nicolò claimed to have met a certain Prince Zichmni and advised him on how to conquer other islands. In 1391, Nicolò's brother Antonio supposedly followed him to Frisland, where, after Nicolò's death, he pursued a fourteen-year-long naval offensive that took him to various other islands, including one allegedly called Estotiland, which was full of large cities and vast quantities of gold. On the accompanying map of the North Atlantic, it is located on the western margin, roughly where Labrador is in eastern Canada.

Did Antonio really reach the American coastline? Or do his descriptions suggest that what he saw must have been some northwestern European island? Nicolò Zeno the Younger claimed to have assembled the book from letters by his forefathers found in a family storage space in Venice. If his account and those of his predecessors are true, then the Zeno brothers would have arrived in North America one hundred years before Columbus. And although the Vikings made it to the continent some four centuries before that, reports of their voyages had not yet reached the rest of Europe. But it is also possible that Nicolò the Elder didn't take part in the voyage at all and was living comfortably in Venice all the while. In fact, recent research suggests that this might be the case. Another question is how much Nicolò the Younger may have edited the surviving fragments of the report.

Yet, questions about its authenticity notwithstanding, the report had a lasting influence. In his 1705 book about Vinland, the Icelandic historian Thormodus Torfaeus asserted that the Zeno report had been invented with the intention of undermining Columbus's fame. In his 1784 *History of Discoveries and Sailing Voyages in the North*, which he was commissioned to write by the Academy of Sciences in St. Petersburg, German naturalist Johann Reinhold Forster (best known for his participation in James Cook's second Pacific voyage) returned to the Zenos' account, passing it on without qualification. Alexander von Humboldt wrote in 1836: "If you examine the Zenos' report with neutrality and an open mind, you find the same love of the truth and detailed description of things, which nothing in Europe could have inspired." Humboldt added: "The facts stand there individually in the report. There is no trace of any sort of accusation and recrimination, so that the suspicion of a swindle is indeed swept aside. Nonetheless, the slight confusion that prevails in the numerical information about distances between places and number of days would seem to attest to the highest disorder in the editing process and the sad state of the manuscripts, which the heirs of the Zenos who made the voyages admitted to partially ripping up because they didn't understand the value and significance of the documents." When he made this statement, Humboldt was perhaps thinking of the declaration, made the previous year by Danish admiral Christian Zahrtmann in *Journal of the Royal Geographic Society*, that the Zenos' book was a "tissue of lies."

Other writings about voyages to the North are also questionable, even if they didn't occasion the same level of controversy. With his *Islandia*, *sive Populorum & mirabilium quae in ea Insula reperiuntur accuratior description* (Iceland or an exact description of the people and miracles to be found there), first published in 1607, the presumably Dutch author Dietmar Blefken promised to shed light upon the island, which he claimed to have visited as a ship's clergyman in 1563. His cultural and moral standards apparently deviated significantly from those of the Icelanders, whom he depicted as superstitious people who believed in magic powers strong enough to stop ships even during fierce winds. But Blefken also wrote of widespread literacy on the island and described the Icelanders as so strong and stout that one man drained a keg of Hamburg beer in a single swallow!

Blefken claimed to have then traveled on to Greenland, where he had been unable to land because his ships couldn't find a port free of ice. Subsequently, he said that he had boarded a Portuguese vessel to Lisbon and then northern Morocco before returning to central Europe. Although Blefken obviously used foreign sources for part of his account, and doubts remain as to whether he actually undertook the voyage he described at all, his book ran through multiple editions and was translated into a number of languages, influencing perceptions of Iceland for centuries. Icelandic humanist Arngrímur Jónsson was so angered by the book that he felt compelled to deny several of its central claims, writing: "Under no circumstances do Icelanders love whoring, drinking, superstition and magic."

Even in accounts of voyages that undoubtedly did happen, there are frequent, obvious mistakes. Such errors may be the product of subsequent editing, conscious embellishment, mistranslations, or simple unconscious human error. As a result, the concrete reality of "the North," at least during earlier centuries, is often difficult to get hold of, running through one's fingers like sand.

What developments inspired the next expeditions to northern oceans? Seafarers from England and the Netherlands focused on the North Atlantic because the southern oceans were dominated by the Spanish and Portuguese, who had accumulated vast wealth and were perceived as a threat. Early explorers were motivated alternately by vague hopes of new natural resources and treasure, new trade possibilities, and open transportation routes that might be shorter than the mid-Atlantic ones dominated by Spain, Portugal, and England.

Sixteenth-century English merchant Robert Thorne was one of the early advocates of exploring the Arctic; conversely and rather naively, he believed that because such routes existed in the south, there had to be passages across the North Pole and the northeastern Atlantic. The seafarer and merchant John Cabot—born Giovanni Caboto in Venice—was likewise convinced that along with the southern route to eastern Asia via the Cape of Good Hope (in South Africa), which had been discovered in 1488, there had to be a corresponding northern "high road." Ultimately, though, he only made it as far as Greenland. In 1497, five years after Columbus landed on a Bahamian island, Cabot nonetheless reached the North American coast during a voyage on behalf of Henry VII. His discovery was crucial in cementing Britain's claim to the territories that would become the United States and Canada.

The achievements of explorers went hand in hand with breakthroughs in cartography and navigation, although maps and navigation aids remained anything but exact by today's standards. On a map by Sebastian Münster from 1588, the countries of northern Europe appear strangely huddled together, as though the oceans surrounding them had shriveled. Southwest of Iceland, you can still see the phantom island of Frisland, which continued to haunt maps for quite some time and which many later writers claimed had to be one of the Faroes. Astonishingly, Münster's map even gave names to places on the fictional island. Another interesting aspect of this map is that, unusual for its time, it puts the north at the bottom.

Along with their hopes for a northwest passage, the English remained obsessed for centuries with the question of whether there was a northern route to China. Playing a major role here was the Venetian seafarer Sebastian Cabot, John Cabot's son, who sailed for many years in the service of the Spanish Crown before eventually returning to England. In 1551, he was named governor of the Muscovy Company, which was specially created to further trade with Russia and compete with the Hanseatic merchants on the Baltic Sea. Extending British activities to northern Russia was supposed to kill two birds with one stone: to gain direct access to Russian goods and to explore possible routes to India and China. The first expeditions to this end suffered horrific losses. Cabot himself died in 1557. But a trading route was discovered across the White Sea. Soon, British explorers arrived on the isle Novaya Zemlya and were able to establish a trading monopoly with Russia.

Dutch ships, also looking for a northeastern passage, advanced into the White Sea on the northwest coast of Russia around the same time and concluded trade agreements on the Kola Peninsula with Novgorodians who had established permanent settlements there. In 1596, Willem Barents, who had been trained in Amsterdam, landed a true coup by discovering the Bjørnøya island above the North Cape and the Svalbard archipelago with its fjords and tundra. (At least, he was the first documented discoverer.) Soon Denmark and Sweden stepped up their interest in the northern Atlantic. At the start of the seventeenth century, Danish-Norwegian King Christian IV commissioned three expeditions to Greenland. Their mission was to identify the best route to the island, find settlers' colonies, and renew Danish territorial claims. But the results were disappointing. The explorers never found out what had happened to colonies established centuries before, and the king abandoned the Greenland project and shifted his activities to the Hudson Bay and the search for a northwest passage. When the Thirty Years' War broke out, Denmark withdrew entirely from high northern waters.

Aside from all the official expeditions, numerous other people voyaged to the northern Atlantic to pursue very concrete interests. Back in the twelfth century, demand grew not only for pelts from the Greenland Vikings, but also for walrus ivory. It was brought back for craftsmen to use to create intricate carvings, prized curios, and symbols of wealth and taste for European "Renaissance men" to display in their collections. With the population of the walruses off the Icelandic coasts dramatically dwindling, Greenland's Scandinavian settlers—as recent Norwegian and British research has shown—succeeded in cornering the European market for ivory for over two centuries. It's possible that they had traded knives and other iron implements with the native Inuit for walrus tusks. In any case, the market abruptly collapsed in the mid-fourteenth century, when the plague broke out in Norway and more and more higher-quality elephant ivory became available from India and Africa.

Whale blubber was also in great demand, since it could be cut into strips and boiled down for what was called "polar oil," to be used in lamps (despite the biting stench when burned). English and Dutch seafarers were particularly interested in blubber. In the sixteenth- and seventeenth-century Netherlands, a flotilla of some three hundred ships and eighteen thousand men was put together to this end. By the second half of the nineteenth century, overfishing had so greatly reduced whale populations that petroleum and kerosene (which is derived from petroleum) became the preferred fuel.

The second most coveted natural resource after whales was cod—a fish that could be easily dried, stored, transported, and then reconstituted with water into something still edible and nutritious. Icelandic fishermen swapped dried cod with Hanseatic merchants for grain, beer, wood, and textiles. As of the sixteenth century, the fish was caught primarily by seamen sailing from the Mediterranean to the northern Atlantic—that was after the Catholic Church began to promote the consumption of fish on Fridays and during Lent, when meat was off-limits. (By contrast, in the early days of Christianity, the fish was a popular symbol of Jesus Christ, and Christians were prohibited from eating it.)

The Portuguese pressed forward as far as Newfoundland in search of cod, which, prepared in a variety of ways, is still considered Portugal's national dish.

Walrus and narwhal ivory wasn't the only material associated with the North. There were also honey-colored, semitransparent, irregular round blobs, sometimes with dead insects and plants inside. At year's end, when the waves were whipped up by what was previously called the "amber wind," such fossil resin was frequently swept off the bottom of the Baltic Sea and washed up on beaches, where it was gathered by "amber catchers." Today we know that this valuable aquatic substance comes from a gigantic forest that covered parts of Scandinavia, the Baltic, and Russia during the Eocene period thirty-four million years ago. Amber is one of the oldest known treasures found in the Baltic region and served as an object of trade and barter up until the Bronze Age. It even found its way to ancient Greece, transported to the Mediterranean from the North and Baltic Seas along two trading routes called the "amber roads" in the eighteenth century.

As much as various nations competed with one another in their northerly voyages of discovery, the success of their endeavors in what was a very alien environment depended on a lively cross-cultural exchange of information. Before his voyages between 1728 and 1741, Denmark's Vitus Bering consulted in St. Petersburg with French cartographer Joseph-Nicolas Delisle, who passed on the information his Parisian colleague Philippe Buache had used to make his maps. Buache's maps were employed by people from other nations as well. Meanwhile, sailing in the service of Russia, Bering discovered the waterway between the northeast of Eurasia and the extreme west of North America that now bears his name.

Little by little, popular knowledge about the North and its denizens coalesced into a somewhat clearer picture, and the image of the Nordic peoples shifted from that of fearsome barbarians to trustworthy merchants with whom good business could be done.

Onerous Journeys to the Lands of the Midnight Sun

E arly central European travelers initially concentrated on the more accessible southern parts of Scandinavia: Denmark, southern and central Sweden, and southern Finland. Norway was less frequently visited. Travelers there mostly came from England because of the close historical and cultural bonds between the two countries. Michael Beheim, who wrote the first German-language account of a maritime voyage to Scandinavia in 1450, remarked that he had never seen "more horrible, wild land" than the Norwegian coast. In his 1646 "Description of the World," influenced by the Thirty Years' War, Gottfried Schultz not only characterized Scandinavians as "coarse and clumsy / mistrustful / sneaky" but also opined: "They think much of themselves / are arrogant / and given to drink. They rarely get sick / have hot bellies / are able to easily digest coarse foods. / They act seriously / and love justice."

As rudimentary, cryptic, and unpolished as they are, these reports of early voyages are valuable. They cover the continually expanding territory of "the North" and serve as tiles in a gradually completed mosaic. Over the centuries, perceptions changed, and voyagers came to organize their written observations in terms of not just chronology, but topics covered. The people they met also learned how better to accommodate visitors, so that the travel experience changed and become more pleasurable. The relatively low population density of Scandinavia meant that its roads and byways were generally far less developed than in western and central Europe. With the exception of Denmark, horses (without carriages) were the sole means of land transportation. Of course, there was often more than one way to get from A to B. To go from Copenhagen to Stockholm, for instance, you could either proceed directly through southern Sweden and travel along the Baltic Sea or take the boat north from Kalmar, across from the isle of Öland, on Sweden's eastern coast.

Traveling in winter had the advantage that ice and snow leveled the uneven and rocky roads. It was easier to make progress across freshly fallen snow. But using sleds, drawn by either horses or reindeer, brought considerable challenges, as described by the polymath Adam Oehlschlegel (latinized Olearius), from the German town of Aschersleben, who traveled in Russia on the other side of the Baltic Sea in 1633: "Because most of our people were unused / to controlling the sled's path and the horse / while sitting in the sleigh / as we had to do back then / we watched as first one then the other repeatedly tipped over / and had to pick himself and his equipment up out of the snow." Moreover, as much as ice sometimes sped up travel, there was the constant danger of breaking through the ice and perishing in freezing waters when crossing lakes or straits. Visitors relied on whatever pelts they could scare up to combat the bitter temperatures, and those who traveled by sled soon discovered how sensible it was to take breaks and walk on foot intermittently to warm up.

Visitors to Scandinavia were impressed by how well its people had adapted to winter, even celebrating several holidays during the cold months. They were astonished, of course, by the sauna culture of the Finns. As Oehlschlaegel noted, they "ran out in the streets from their bathhouses in the depths of winter / rubbed themselves down with snow / and then ran back inside to the warmth," suffering no noticeable ill effects from the "rapid alternation between heat and cold."

Not all encounters with the winter cold were voluntary, as exemplified by the fate of Johann Eberhard Zetzner, who en route from Amsterdam to Gdansk (the Baltic coast city in what is now Poland) was shipwrecked in the Skagerrak, which was notorious for its fierce storms. He was forced to spend the winter of 1669–1670 in southern Norway. As contemporary historian Sascha Taetz relates in his study of sixteenth- and seventeenth-century travelogues written by private city dwellers, Zetzner shared his quarters "with a Frenchman forced to flee his native land because of duels, a Pole, a scholar from Riga, a Livonian, a Saxon, a citizen of Kraków and a refugee not described in any further detail."

In any case, Zetzner got a chance to experience the surely unforgettable thrill of traveling by sled across the frozen Arendal Sound to the nearby town of Christianssand, his route lit by torches, since it was "no longer light for more than four or five hours a day." No doubt the Protestant Norwegian hosts must have rubbed their eyes when their stranded winter visitors staged a Carnival parade dressed up in bearskins and East Indian sailor's outfits. The "people of the North," Zetzner wrote, "could rarely be seen on the street and stuck to . . . their houses."

Temperatures, of course, do not depend on latitude alone, and many travelers during the summer months were surprised when what they experienced didn't match their expectations. How many of them reckoned with the searing rays of the sun and the clouds of tiny biting insects in the tundra? Or that they could get a sunburn on days that started out with frost?

Norway's numerous mountains and lakes often reminded voyagers of Switzerland. A young merchant named Samuel Kiechel, from the city of Ulm in southwestern Germany, also drew additional parallels in his 1586 travelogue. In both Norway and Switzerland, the people were "strong, hardworking and coarse," and their farmers spoke a "rough tongue" and made "really powerful cheese." Other writers speculated that the Swiss might well be descendants of the Swedes. Moreover, Stockholm and Venice were frequently mentioned in the same breath, even if they had little more in common than being located on the ocean and built atop pillars. The Protestant polymath Martin Zeiler, from the Steiermark region of Austria, wrote in 1647 that the Swedish capital was "just like Venice," constructed "amidst puddles." He could well have gotten this idea from the famous mapmaker Sebastian Münster, since he had never actually been in either city.

The first goal of all voyages to the European North was to reach the mainland of the Scandinavian Peninsula. Larger cargo ships were a popular means of travel, since the small barges typical of northern lands offered practically no protection against the elements, and swabs often had both hands full trying to bail them out and keep them from sinking during fierce rainstorms. There was always the threat of being blown off course on longer sea voyages, and schedules were unpredictable. Wherever they could, ships sailed near land, so it was sometimes possible to go ashore, spend the night, and stock up on fresh water and food. The narrow passages through the Baltic Sea's thousands of skerries, tiny rocky islands, were notorious, and in places sailors could almost reach out and touch the surrounding cliffs. Adolf Nicklass zu Steinkallenfels, who sailed from the Åland Islands to Åbo in Finland in 1615, couldn't conceal his amazement at the division of nautical labor between the sexes, in which the women steered the ship while the men went fishing and hunting.

Although Sweden had established its reputation as a civilized place that was no longer the cradle of evil—one that even became a major European power under King Gustavus Adolphus—it still took some convincing to dispel prejudices about the extreme High North. Danish pastor Lucas Jacobson Debes spent two decades on the Faroe Islands and in 1673 published a work entitled *Færoæ & Færoa reserata*, published in English three years later as *A Description of the Islands & Inhabitants of Foeroe*. He wrote:

> As for what concerneth the good, though one might think in other places, that these Islands being so far remote, there should live in them a rude and barbarous people; notwithstanding one may in truth write of them, that for the Countreys conveniency, they are not only understanding people, and skill'd in their Laws, but also much more civil then Peasants use to be in other parts: who nevertheless

see every day more gentleness amongst those that live in Towns, then this Country can afford. For they are humble in their Conversation, civil in their carriage, and courteous in their speech; specially towards strangers, and those that are better then themselves: they are serviceable, obedient, willing, and liberal to their Magistrates; and those of Feroe must be praised above many other Nations in this, that a stranger travelling through the Land, not only is well received by them, and treated with the best they have, without paying any thing; but also, when they depart, if the Host is able, are gratified with a present, and besides helped with free carriage to the next habitation; which happeneth here, because it is not so ordinary for strangers to travel over the Land, as in other Countreys; for if it were so, they would be obliged to become of the same mind as others.

The Italian priest Francesco Negri was among the earliest explorers to consciously set his sights on Lapland, a region claimed territorially by Denmark-Norway, Sweden, and Russia and which as yet didn't have any clear borders. From the start, it was his aim to reach the North Cape. Driven by limitless curiosity about the "land of the midnight sun," in 1663 he set out from Ravenna for Denmark and pressed on to the northern Swedish Torne River, which forms a large part of Sweden's border with Finland, before the onset of winter forced him to return to Stockholm. The following spring, badly prepared for the trip, he took off again for Lapland. Along the way people repeatedly saved his life. In his posthumously published 1700 travelogue *Viaggio Settentrionale* (trip to the North), he wrote of the simple life and kindness of the Sámi (or Laps or Laplanders, as they used to be called)— a seminomadic people best known for their reindeer herding: "It's true that the Laplanders don't live in palaces, but they also have no worries that those palaces could come down on their heads one day. They also have no fears of losing splendor and fame, of which they know nothing. In all these respects, the Laplanders are better philosophers than Diogenes who, after all, wanted an entire barrel to himself. They are content with even less."

Although Negri's depiction of the Sámi was overwhelmingly positive, his mention of their shamans allegedly praying to the devil did cast a dark shadow. Negri continued to travel for the rest of the year. It wasn't until the winter of 1666 that he reached the North Cape, the long-anticipated destination of his three-year journey. He wrote: "I'm here at the North Cape on the edge of Finnmark [a region in northernmost Norway] and with that the edge of the world, for there are no more places inhabited by men north of here. I am satisfied that I have reached this place and shall return to Denmark, and God willing, the country of my birth."

Another of the travelogues of these years was the Latin-language *Lapponia* of 1673 by the humanist Johannes Scheffer, a German who made his voyages under the Swedish flag. His work was quickly translated into English, German, French, and Dutch and attracted a broad audience. It promised that "rather then [sic] in America, we have a new World discovered; and those extravagant falsehoods, which have commonly past [sic] in the narratives of these Northern countries, are not so inexcusable for their being lies, as that they were told without temtation [sic]; the real truth being equally entertaining, and incredible." The hopes for detailed descriptions of the mystical powers and many heathen customs among the Laplanders that Scheffer also mentioned likely spurred this work's popularity. Did their mystical powers allow them to draw milk from reindeer and hitch them to sleighs? Were the Sámi really able to summon the wind and calm it back down by manipulating unseen forces?

In 1707, a man named Nicolaus Örn, born in the northern Swedish region of Norrbotten, published his *Brief Description of Lapland*. He introduced himself in the third person: "This Laplander / by the name of Nicolaus Örn / in anno 1702 at the age of 20 and in the desire to see foreign countries / indeed as the first of his kind undertook a trip / through Sweden / Dennemark / Germany / and Italy to Rome. / In all the places he passed through / in which no one had ever seen a Laplander / he in his Lapland clothing / awakened amazement." During his journey, Örn no doubt profited from the interest Scheffer's book had elicited and attracted attention to himself with his exotic garb. Örn's brief tract depicted the Sámi far more realistically than Scheffer had, writing that they were now Lutherans, "no longer as irrational and heathen as they had been," although still "prone to superstition." Örn also characterized them as honest in character, even if their external appearance didn't really conform with accepted ideas about truly civilized people. Whether Örn—who came to describe himself as "the Prince of Lapland"—truly was a Sámi is impossible to know; he might have "just" been a Swede who had observed Sámi people in his homeland.

A good example of how alien Sweden could appear even to an educated Swede and how wild the country's North still was in the eighteenth century is seen in *Lachesis Lapponica: A Tour in Lapland,* by the naturalist Carl Linnaeus, an obsessive collector and cataloger who made a crucial contribution to the scientific classification of plants and animals. In May 1732, having just turned 25, he set off north, "swept away by an unbelievable longing for the Lapland mountains" on the margins of Sweden. His travelogue minutely chronicles his progress from Uppsala to "Lappmark," registering the flora, fauna, and stones he observed down to the smallest detail. Linnaeus's work is a naturalist-ethnographic inventory of the landscape interspersed with opaque Latin vocabulary. Significantly, his sense of being in alien territory didn't first begin in Lapland. He was also struck by the remarkable characteristics of Swedish and Norwegian farmers, who, for instance, baked a bitter sort of bread with flour made of the ground bark of pine trees. Linnaeus carefully observed the Sámi's complex codependence on reindeer, their wedding rituals, their bear hunts, their typical illnesses and treatments thereof, and the special dietary habits maintained by this short-statured people. "I saw not a single person who was as large as I am," Linnaeus wrote, adding, "I have never seen a Laplander with a fat stomach. The milk also makes him supple." The naturalist concluded that well concealed "in the hindermost corner of the world," the Sámi were thoroughly contented people. "You live out your years without care until you're over a hundred, remaining fit until old age and in excellent health. . . . You live in your forests like the birds, who neither sow nor reap, to whom all-merciful God grants enough to eat."

The extended lonely forests of the North also contained a whole world of animal species. What about the small animals living in the Lapland mountains, of which it was said in Norway dropped like rain from the clouds? Linnaeus took it upon himself to discredit this bizarre legend. The only

Carol Linnaeus in Lappish dress with one of his favorite flowers, the twinflower. *Carolus Linnaeus (1707–1778) in Lappish dress. Oil painting after Martin Hoffman. Wellcome Collection*

evidence he could find of such creatures was an illustration of *Mus nor-vegicus* in Ole Worm's 1653 *Historia Naturalis*—which speculated that the creature might have arisen in the clouds. Linnaeus wrote of these animals' behavior: "They are not particularly fearsome. On the contrary they bark like a young dog when approached too closely. They are bold enough to bite the stick if they're poked, and tend not to run away."

Linnaeus also reported that these "mice," actually lemmings (now called

Sámi people in Lapland as shown in a nineteenth-century German educational
picture book. Lemmings appear in the foreground. *Wagner, Hermann.* Naturgemälde der
ganzen Welt. *Esslingen: Verlag von J. F. Schreiber, 1869*

Lemmus lemmus), occasionally set off in great numbers and ran to their deaths—which is the basis of the ineradicable myth of the creatures committing "mass suicide." (Today we know that lemmings' behavior is an impulse to frantically look for new habitats in response to overpopulation, during which some of the creatures lose their bearings.) Linnaeus climbed a number of the highest Lapland mountains, above the cloud line, and could attest with great certainty that, superstition notwithstanding, animals and people were not borne away by the clouds that surrounded them "like a thick fog." He wrote: "If you enter into mist so thick that you can no longer make out the snow on the ground, it is easy to fall into a chasm carved out by water and get buried. That is the origin of the talk that the clouds carry off Laplanders along with their reindeer and toss them down from the mountains. The same is true of these mice, which like other animals born and bred in these mountains, descend from them in great colonies during certain years."

Linnaeus's journey lasted six months, during which time he covered more than 1,200 miles and inventoried some one hundred plants he later included in his *Flora Lapponica*. Astonished, he wrote that he sometimes felt he might as well have been in "Africa or Asia—since the geology, the situation and the plants were completely unknown to me."

Northern Wonderland

"Now I must report something about a strange, unheard-of phenomenon, or sign in the air, namely the so-called northern light or northern shine, which can be seen in a variety of very different guises during winter nights in this northern world and which often attracted my attention and made me observe and gaze upon it for long stretches of time. . . . I know of no more vivid description and depiction of this phenomenon than to call it bright, illuminated clouds that, quicker than you realize, transform from one shape to another and even after they appear, don't begin and end at any one particular point in time."

Such were the words of the German classical philologist Immanuel Johann Gerhard Scheller, who worked as a teacher in Stockholm and traveled to Lapland in the early eighteenth century. He speculated that the cause of the "heavenly shine" he observed there had to do with the somewhat more elevated position of the sun during winter and reflections from the snow. One of the wildest explanations for the northern lights was the theory formulated in 1714 by British astronomer Edmond Halley, who assumed that Earth was hollow and that there was an opening near the North Pole, from which light poured out from the planet's core. Absurd as that idea may seem, this was one of the first times someone had drawn a connection between Earth's magnetic field and the northern lights. Only later would scientists understand that the eruptions on the surface of the sun produced solar winds that collided with Earth's magnetic field, bringing together terrestrial and extraterrestrial matter and sometimes unleashing the spectacle that has been compared to a heavenly dance of veils.

The fact that the sky barely got dark during Scandinavia's short summer was considered something just shy of a miracle. "No darkness and night for the whole summer, no intolerable heat from the sun, healthy, temperate air, and *in summa* everything fresh, cheerful, peaceful and calm," rhapsodized Olaus Magnus. Early travelers remarked that they were able to read letters at midnight even during the new moon and "could count money nearly the whole night through." Johann Gerhard Scheller, who was fascinated by the northern lights, reported hearing that "the sun never sets in the summer" in the northern Swedish city of Torneå—something he claimed to have confirmed with his own eyes. In his travelogue, Scheller precisely recorded the times of sunrises and sunsets. The differences in the durations of days and nights in the North was a great mystery. Baron August zu Mörsberg, who undertook a journey to the Nordic countries in 1592, thought that astronomers "who are better acquainted with the course of the heavens and stars like the sun and moon" should provide answers. He added: "During our Norwegian and Swedish journey, there was no order to our midday meals or night camps. After traveling for an hour, or four or five, whenever we were hungry, thirsty or tired, we looked for a nice spot or bit of the brush, removed the exquisite bridles and bits from our horses and let them look for feed themselves. . . . When we were sleepy, we'd lie down for an hour, or three or four, without waiting for nightfall, since the sun shone all day where we were. Night comes rarely and, even then, only for half an hour to an hour."

Another treasure attracting great interest were the runes discovered on many large upright stones, particularly in Sweden. In 1594, the linguist Johan Bure (Johannes Bureus), who grew up near Uppsala, began to study this writing. Shortly before the turn of the next century, the Swedish Crown commissioned him to journey throughout the country and gather comprehensive impressions, which he documented in a book. The task into which Bure threw himself wasn't a purely scientific one. His fascination with runes stemmed from his idea of replacing the Latin alphabet with the older, mystic letters. Although he was unsuccessful in this, his 1611 book *Runa-ABC-boken* was the first in Swedish on the topic of alphabets. At this juncture we again encounter Ole Worm, who, after Bure, was at the time the most important scholar of runes. To research his compendium of Danish rune stones, which he published in 1643 as *Danicorum Momentorum Libri Sex*, Worm sent artists out throughout the Danish kingdom to draw up an inventory. He wanted to prove his fantastic hypothesis that early Scandinavian literature had been composed in a rune alphabet derived from the Hebrew one.

So what *is* the story behind the runes? Today we know that the rune alphabet was used from at least the second to the eighteenth centuries, most recently in rune books, but that most of the well-known rune writings date from the Viking era. There are various hypotheses on their possible origin, but one common element is that they were based on a southern European model, be it the Latin, Greek, or Italian-Etruscan alphabet. And although the symbols chiseled into stone or carved in wood are surrounded by an aura of mystery and profundity, the writings are often about relatively prosaic concerns, remembering the deceased or recording ordinary events. The highly ornamented Täby runestone north of Stockholm reads simply: "Torkel and Fulluge erected this runestone and also the bridge named for their father Sten. Olev made the runes."

Far more significant for later centuries' cultural understanding of northern Europe than the decipherment of the mysterious runestones were the translations of Old Norse writings. As early as the sixteenth century, the humanist scholars of the Norwegian town of Bergen—Scandinavia's largest city well into the following century—labored over editions of these documents in "dansk," the written language of the Danes and Norwegians at the time. (Today, Norwegians call Dano-Norwegian "bokmål" as opposed to "landsmål" or, unofficially "nynorsk," which is a synthetic Norwegian based on Norwegian dialects and was introduced during the National Romantic period.) There is also evidence of seventeenth-century English writers and scholars' interest in these writings. One of them was Sir Henry Spelman, who corresponded with Ole Worm and took information about runes back with him to England to use for historical research and writing.

Apart from runestones, artifacts of the Indigenous populations didn't attract much interest from the explorers and colonialists before the late nineteenth century, at which point people began to collect and take them home for the natural history museums springing up in many cities of the Western world. A fascinating example of artifacts of the Indigenous cultures across the Arctic are maps in a variety of shapes and materials. Maps sometimes were oral descriptions; at other times they were carved in ice and thus ephemeral.

The Dane Gustav Holm, who explored the Ammassalik coast of eastern Greenland, encountered many Inuit communities, and discovered a number of ice fjords in the 1880s, was fascinated by maps carved in wood and collected them. These long, three-dimensional objects showed the irregularities of the alternating fingers of land and fjord of this unique coastline. They were designed to be touched and served mostly as storytelling aids, not for practical navigational use. And they helped to communicate knowledge about certain areas and strengthened human relationships with both land and sea. A hunter and native from the settlement of Umivik by the name of Kunit is known to have sold a set of these "maps" to Holm, who then gave them to the National Museum of Denmark in Copenhagen (where Ole Worm's cabinet is also found). In the mid-1960s, the maps became part of the collection of the Greenland National Museum, in Nuuk.

Tired of the South

The New Love Affair with the North

Although the focus of this book isn't on changes in the political constellations in northern Europe, it's worth noting that national boundaries continued to fluctuate for a long time and were only consolidated in the nineteenth and twentieth centuries. Until 1860, southern Sweden was part of Denmark. Norway first formed a union with Denmark in 1536, and they formed an integrated state in 1660; then after the Napoleonic Wars, it was ceded to Sweden. Meanwhile, Denmark kept control of the Faroe Islands, Iceland, and Greenland. Before becoming independent in 1917, Finland was part of first Sweden, then Russia. Not to disregard tensions and differences, but the history of the countries of northern Europe reveals their cultural connectedness. Moreover, the northern hinterlands of the European continent often barely registered in the consciousness of the educated elites in London, Paris, and Berlin. Norway was seen as a narrow, inaccessible strip of land, populated only along the coast. Northern

Sweden was of little significance at all, and most people didn't know how far the country actually extended. The mental "map" of northern Europe in the minds of sophisticated people in the early modern era was quite different than ours today.

In 1696, German philosopher and mathematician Gottfried Wilhelm Leibniz wrote in an essay on language: "Everything the Swedes, Norwegians and Icelanders claim for their Goths and runes is ours, and they work on our behalf with all of their efforts, however admirable, for they cannot be considered anything but northern Germans, and were indeed counted among the Germans by well-informed Tacitus and all the Antique and medieval authors. With their language, they prove nothing other than this, no matter how they twist and turn. I can conclude from a number of circumstances that in the waning days of the Empire, the Danes were known to the Romans as Saxons."

By drawing an explicit connection between the Germans and their northern neighbors, Leibniz paved the way for what would come later. Previously, Scandinavia hadn't been in the frame when people talked about the ancient German past.

Although the intellectual traditions of the Mediterranean remained important, Rome hadn't been the capital of the world for quite some time, and Italy and Greece were generally becoming less significant. Most modern thinkers came from farther north and west: France, German-speaking Europe, the Netherlands, and England. The result was a reimagination, a new mental mapping of the European continent.

Discovering
the Norse Myths

S tarting in 1755, the Geneva historian Paul Henri Mallet began publishing his multivolume history of the "religion, laws, customs and
habits of the early Danes." Forming a part of his *Introduction à l'histoire de
Dannemarc* were Old Norse tales written down in the thirteenth century,
including the *Prose Edda* and excerpts from the *Poetic Edda* from Iceland,
both of which feature Scandinavian divine and heroic themes. The *Prose
Edda* is also known as the *Snorra Edda* after a certain Snorri Sturluson,
who in Iceland set about trying to write a primer for poets, so-called skalds,
to cite mythological verses. The *Poetic Edda* collected whole songs and
poems by unknown authors, encompassing fifteen Nibelungen songs from
an epic poem written around 1200. Crucially, these texts were recorded in
Christianized Iceland and influenced by that faith.

Mallet made use, among other things, of centuries-old Latin versions of
the ancient texts by Thomas Bartholin, Ole Worm, and Peder Resen and

translated them into French. Soon after, his work was itself translated into English, Danish, German, Russian, and Polish, making the ancient texts accessible to broad audiences for the first time. This was the beginning of a resurgence of interest abroad in all things coming from Scandinavia and Iceland. "Germany" at this point still consisted of a collection of individual, often small-scale states. A unified German nation would not be formed until almost a century later, but one could herald the *Edda* as an "Armory of a new German genius," as did the German philosopher Johann Gottfried Herder after he read Mallet's book with great enthusiasm. For him, that created a sense of belonging to an imagined homeland in the North. The euphoric Herder felt he was entering new territory: Old Norse mythology as an alternative to a stale classicism that venerated Greco-Roman legends and myths. Many people at the time were sick of the South. While Herder was opposed to the idea of distinct races, he was convinced that one human race had diversified into different cultures: "In all the different forms in which the human race appears on earth, it is nonetheless everywhere one and the same human species." However, this sort of "cultural pluralism" didn't save Herder from thinking in racist categories; he asked his readers "to sympathize with the Negro, but not despise him, since the conditions of his climate could not grant him nobler gifts." He had few sympathies with the Chinese, "who, in their own corner of the earth, refrained, like the Jews, from mixing with other peoples." And the high number of composite characters would help to keep them in "childish captivity."

Herder tossed around terms like "German, "Teutonic," "Germanic," "Gothic," "Nordic," "northernly," "Celtic," and "Scandinavian" with aban-don, as though he could recognize the story of German origins in Old Norse mythology. Thus, he inspired the ideological fascination of later writers with the notion of early Germanic tribes originating in the Far North. Although Herder himself never ventured above Riga (today the cap-ital of the Baltic state of Latvia), he had a clear image of the North in mind: "This is where the miracles of our earthy creation are to be seen, such as no inhabitant at the equator would believe, those huge masses of beautiful colored clumps of ice, those majestic northern lights, wonderful tricks of eye thanks to the air and in the great cold up there the oft warm fissures in the earth." Herder reprised the comparisons with Alpine Europe from early travelogues not just in physical terms, but as moral standard: "Like in a northern Switzerland, the simplicity of original German virtues has long been preserved and will persist after they are only the stuff of old legend in Germany itself."

The "northern air," Herder believed, gave the ancient German tribesmen their strength. In his 1774 book *Another Philosophy of History for the Education of Mankind*, he wrote: "A new man was born in the North. Under the fresh skies, in the desert and the wilderness, a springtime of strong, nutritious plants—planted in the lovelier, more southern lands—now sad empty fields!—that took on a new nature and that should yield a mighty harvest for the destiny of the world!"

It's easy to lose your way in Herder's verbose, hyperactive effusiveness. But his rejection of the genealogy of Noah in his *Ideas for the Philosophy of the History of Humanity* was unambiguous: "The various efforts of people to make all nations of the earth, according to this genealogy, into descendants of the Hebrews and half-brothers of the Jews, contradicts not only chronology and the entire history of humanity but also the standpoint of this narrative itself. . . . Enough of it! The fixed center of the largest part of the world, the primeval mountains of Asia, provided the first place of residence for the human race."

For Herder there were two basic coordinates: the North and Asia. Beyond Germany, he was an important force in paving the way for the categories "Aryan" and "Semitic" that, as Maurice Olender stressed in *The Languages of Paradise* (1993), "would influence scholarship in the human sciences throughout the nineteenth century." Herder's Indophilia took up strands of thought from Leibniz and spun them out even further. He found a spiritual ally in Friedrich Schlegel, who had learned some Sanskrit during a stay in Paris and who declared at an 1805 lecture, "Everything absolutely everything, comes from India!" Schlegel also revived the term *Aryan* as a combination of the Sanskrit name Ari (meaning, among other things, lion, brave, inner skin, and eagle) with the German word *Ehre* (honor). The concept can be traced back to the eighteenth-century French Orientalist Abraham-Hyacinthe Anquetil-Duperron, who coined it in his translation of the Avesta, the holy book of Zoroastrianism. It was subsequently adopted by linguists in various countries.

Schlegel saw the "Germanic feeling for nature" in the teachings concerning Norse gods and in the *Poetic Edda*—he called them the "northern core." For Schlegel there was no contradiction at all to speculations that such writings originated in Persia or India. Leaving aside the extremely tenuous nature of the presumed connections between the *Edda* and prehistorical myths and cults, Norse divinities had certain affinities with those of Antiquity, even if their image was repeatedly altered after being copied again and again over the course of centuries.

The poet and Orientalist August Wilhelm Schlegel, Friedrich's brother, associated the East with religion as "the region of expectation—the eternal dawn is its symbol." By contrast, the West stood for morality as "that heavenly direction that brings images of rest and satisfaction after a good day's work," while he attributed to the South "the piquant, thrilling products of the fine arts that can only be drawn out by heat and the charming summer." The North was altogether different: "The North is science, the very picture of strictness and gravity. The immobile North Star that guides seafarers is there. And the magnet points north—the greatest symbol of the immutability and identity of self-consciousness that is the foundation of all science, all philosophical evidence."

Along with the *Poetic* and *Prose Edda*, a number of European writers and scholars became interested in the Icelandic sagas in the late eighteenth century: written narratives of conflicts that often end dramatically or tragically and are set in the days soon after Iceland was first settled. The word *saga* is derived from the Old West Norse verb *segia*, meaning "to say" or "to tell." We cannot reconstruct who first wrote the sagas or later revised them. They are not absolutely authentic, as they were repeatedly altered by diligent monks to better conform with Christianity—a fact conveniently ignored by their fans, who wanted to see them as genuine. In any case, the popularity of ancient Icelandic writings fulfilled Scandinavians' age-old dream of finally being recognized internationally and no longer dismissed as a cultural and intellectual backwater.

The new myth of the lively, invigorating North dovetailed with physical and astrological topics popular at the time. Ideas of "astral forces," of magnetism, electricity, and phenomena of illumination like the northern lights and the North Star gave the North a mysterious nimbus. Scholars drew bold parallels.

By no means was the entire German intelligentsia of the day equally susceptible to enthusiasm for the North. Many learned people consciously maintained distance to Iceland and Scandinavia; nothing, they thought, could have come from the region as significant as had come from Greece and Italy. August Ludwig von Schlözer made no secret of the fact that he did not hold the Old Norse writings in very high regard, dismissing the *Poetic Edda* on numerous occasions as a "notorious relic" no better than a fairy tale. Johann Wolfgang von Goethe—that great embodiment of German culture—was also immune to the "dream of the North in German intellectual life," as Danish literary historian Carl Roos characterized this wave of enthusiasm in 1967. While Goethe recognized the value of the *Edda*, he saw nothing in it that could inspire major innovations in modern literature. "I was glad to have consumed my inherited northern portion and then move on to the table of the Greeks," he remarked, succinctly and cuttingly, to his confidante Johann Peter Eckermann in 1826. In his biography *Poetry and Truth*, Goethe wrote: "What now could have induced me to substitute Wotan for Jupiter, and Thor for Mars, and instead of the precisely described southern figures, to introduce shapes in the mist, mere verbal sounds, into my poetic works?" Goethe felt greater affinity with the wisdom of the Parsis from Persia. That notwithstanding, early in his career and certainly not out of nowhere, Goethe composed his melancholy 1774 ballad "The King in Thule," which would later be set to music by Franz Schubert.

While Norse mythology circulated among European writers, it was not widely known at the time, not even in northern Europe: As late as 1801, Danish historian Jens Möller compared Norse mythology with "a newly

discovered land of flowers which no botanist has yet examined carefully and most of whose blossoms have thus not yet been brought into a
system—by contrast the flowers of Greek mythology have been allocated
to their specific genus and species for centuries." In 1801, the University of
Copenhagen announced an essay competition on the topic "Would it be
profitable for the literature of the northern countries if our writers adopted
and generally used the old Norse mythology instead of the Greek?"

Another intellectual who shook up European understanding of "the
North," in a different way though, was Schlözer. He spent many years in
Stockholm and Uppsala, during which time he made the acquaintance of
Linnaeus and learned Swedish, Icelandic, and Sámi. Schlözer characterized Finland as the "Canada of Europe" and the Sámi as "a true Bedouin
source of pride." Even though he gave his 1771 book *General Northern History* the subtitle *For a Correct Understanding of all Scandinavian, Finnish, Slavic, Latvian and Siberian Peoples,* he knew how presumptuous he
was being: "If a historian in Uppsala or Moscow were to attempt to unify
the pasts of the Portuguese, Spanish, French, Italians, Germans, Dutch,
Swiss, English, Scots and Irish within a single 'History of the South,' he
would attract stares of disbelief, and people would find his use of the term
bizarre. Do we not do likewise when we speak of northern history, as I
do out of respect for the common use of language, when we toss together
Danes, Norwegians, Icelanders, Swedes, Poles, Russians, Prussians, Lithua-
nians, Latvians, Livonians, Curonians, Finns and Laplanders into one class
of people and try to understand them all under a single, generic, purely
geographical name?"

A Confidence Man
and a Blind Bard

Dark clouds brewing up in the sky, fog rolling in, swords rattling, warriors battling, and the sun and moon conjuring up dramatic effects—these ingredients so familiar from the genre of fantasy literature were also hallmarks of one of the most famous frauds in literary history: the *Works of Ossian*, presumed to be the creation of a third-century Scottish bard, Ossian, writing about his father, King Fingal. The collection was first published in 1765 by Scotsman James Macpherson, a native Gaelic speaker. Five years earlier, in 1760, Macpherson had made a name for himself with *Fragments of Ancient Poetry—Collected in the Highlands of Scotland and Translated from the Gaelic or Erse Language*. Many Scots had longed for the discovery of a Scottish national epic, and Macpherson tried to fulfill that desire, making several trips to the Highlands and searching energetically, but in vain, for traces of such a work. So he did the best with what he had and invented the *Works of Ossian*.

It wasn't long after these works were published that no less a scholar than the English writer Samuel Johnson wrote critically about them. Johnson didn't just doubt their authenticity. He went so far as to question whether a serious written culture had ever existed in the Scottish Highlands, adding, "Nor are their primitive customs and ancient manner of life otherwise than very faintly and uncertainly remembered by the present race." In short, Johnson refused to acknowledge Macpherson's "discovery" for the simple reason that it came from Scotland. There was nothing that could have changed his preference for the traditions of the South, as he stated in 1776: "A man who has not been in Italy is always conscious of an inferiority, from his not having seen what it is expected a man should see. The grand object of travelling is to see the shores of the Mediterranean. On those shores were the four great empires of the world: the Assyrian, the Persian, the Grecian, and the Roman. All our religion, almost all our law, almost all our arts, almost all that sets us above savages, has come to us from the shores of the Mediterranean."

However, Macpherson's audience, hungry for nostalgia, had no qualms about the genuineness of his bathetic, confusing verses. His melancholy verses matched the mood of the times. The author achieved fame and fortune, was celebrated as a national hero, and at the end of his life was given a state funeral. It wasn't until 1807, eleven years after his death, that it was conclusively proved that the works of Ossian, though based to a small extent on surviving Celtic fragments and motifs, were fake.

The Hebrides, off the northwest Scottish coast, played a major role in this fiction, as Scotland, which had unified with England in 1707, began to attract more tourist interest. Influential travelogues, such as Thomas Pennant's 1769 *A Tour in Scotland*, accompanied the discovery of Scotland as a picturesque destination, and not only because of its natural beauty. The universities of Aberdeen, St. Andrews, Edinburgh, and Glasgow also appealed to the intellectually curious. Ossian's disciples soon found a suitable place of pilgrimage on Staffa, an uninhabited island in the Inner Hebrides and home to Fingal's Cave, a cavern surrounded by geometrically formed basalt pillars with the sea roaring at its entrance. Legend has it that they were erected by Macpherson's King Fingal—and they inspired Felix Mendelssohn Bartholdy's concert overture *The Hebrides*. The cave had been rediscovered by naturalist Sir Joseph Banks in 1772.

Napoleon Bonaparte, another admirer of Macpherson's forgery, commissioned a painting featuring Ossian motifs for his bedroom.

Meanwhile, Herder, who lamented the fact that Germans had no Ossian of their own, long dreamed of traveling to England and Scotland, writing in a 1773 letter: "O friend, you have no idea how much stock I put at one time in this Scotsman. One glance, I thought, at the open spirit and the stage and the whole lively theater of the English people [would suffice] to clear away entirely the dark and strange ideas, so confusing, that arise in a foreign mind about the history, philosophy, politics and unique features of this wonderful nation."

Herder never undertook any such trip. The German writers Friedrich Gottlieb Klopstock, Gotthold Ephraim Lessing, Friedrich Schiller, and Ludwig Tieck were also among the fans of Ossian. Franz Schubert was inspired to write eleven songs—songs of lamentation honoring dead heroes—based on Ossian texts, and the youthful Goethe included prose translations of them in his *Sorrows of Young Werther*. The protagonist Werther reads from them to his beloved, Lotte, exclaiming, "In my heart Ossian has displaced Homer. What a world into which the magnificent poet leads me!" Goethe's novel did much to enhance the popularity of Macpherson's forgery. Even Thomas Jefferson was cited as saying, "I am not ashamed to own that I think this rude bard of the North the greatest Poet that has ever existed."

So in Great Britain, Macpherson's Ossian created waves that the Old Norse writings had not been able to generate, although many of them had already been translated. Among English writers, William Blake represented—as he so often did—the exception, one of the very few Englishmen fascinated by Old Norse writings, although we don't know the true depth of interest. In any case, he worked a number of Old Norse motifs into his writings and his visual works, for instance, in his illustrations for

Thomas Gray's *The Descent of Odin*. The powerful female voices from Gray's odes are echoed in Blake's own poetry. In his *Marginalia*, he exhorts his audience, "Read the Edda of Iceland!" It was an attempt to repudiate the claim of his contemporary theologians that the peoples who lived prior to Christianity had no ethical sense.

The Scent of the Arctic

A t the turn of the nineteenth century, more and more people were no longer content to learn about the North from the comfort of their reading chairs and were willing to get their shoes a bit muddy to see it for themselves, both scientists and more romantic travelers. This was partly because the French Revolution made it more difficult and sometimes impossible to travel to central Europe, whereas English and German travelers could reach Scandinavia and Scotland without any great problem. Increasingly, tourists began visiting the North rather than the sites of antique culture in Italy and Greece. To stand in the Roman Forum as the first Caesar Augustus did or, by visiting the ruins of Pompeii, to come into contact with one of the most dramatic natural disasters of antique Italy had lost some of its appeal. While some of the travelers followed in the footsteps of the great Linnaeus, others, among them readers of the Genevan philosopher Jean-Jacques Rousseau, were hoping to find people in a "state of nature"—noble savages. Or they had heard about the wonders of the midnight sun and the majestic fjords of Norway.

Hardly anyone justified his trip as clearly as the British naturalist Edward Daniel Clarke, who began his journey through Europe in 1799 starting in Norway and Sweden. The voyage was conceived as a repudiation of some of his contemporaries. In the Scandinavian section of his 1816 book *Travels in Various Countries of Europe, Asia and Africa,* he pointed out that the lands of the North were "countries seldom seen by literary men; and, at this time, less liable than any other to those political convulsions which agitated more frequented regions." Earlier in his life, Clarke had already written that Italy, "exhausted by a long and successful scrutiny, is unable to supply new gratification, either in art or antiquity." Now he wanted to expose himself to the influences of Scandinavia's many facets, its "wild and romantic scenery, and the unsophisticated character of its inhabitants"— farmers, fishermen, and hunters. After his travel companions William Otter and Thomas Malthus decided to head home upon reaching Sweden's Lake Vänern, he pressed on with the words, "I do not intend to turn back until I have scented the polar air."

Clarke was a passionate collector of plants, historical manuscripts, old medals, minerals, costumes, and animal pelts, including those of a Norwegian lynx, a mountain squirrel, a white fox, and a reindeer. He was captivated by the North in all its facets. Was the British and English past, which people considered lost, still on evidence in Norway like in a living museum? English travelers thought so. They often found that they rarely had difficulties making themselves understood to people in that country or the neighboring one. "In the Swedish I behold the origin of my native language, somewhat corrupted in Norway, and almost obliterated in England," wrote Clarke.

These thoughts didn't come from nowhere, of course. The Anglo-Saxons and the Scandinavians had long-standing historical connections, beginning with the settlement of the northeastern third of the present-day United Kingdom by Scandinavians in the ninth century. The Danelaw—the name of this part of the country—was ruled by the Norse and governed by

Norse laws. This is reflected in English place names, most notably York, and extensive archaeological finds have demonstrated the huge influence of Norse culture on the history of Great Britain. Many English words are borrowed directly from Old Norse, including "husband" (*húsbóndi*), "ransack" (*rannsaka*), "slaughter" (*slatra*), and "egg," which is exactly the same in both languages.

Nonetheless, it is tough to say precisely how much influence the language spoken in Scandinavia may have had on Anglo-Saxon Old English, since, as Germanic tongues, both share common central European roots. Nor do we know how long pockets of Scandinavian culture and language survived in mainland Britain. The exception is the Orkney and Shetland Islands, which used to belong to Norway. There, the Norn idiom, which is considered a North Germanic language, was spoken up until the eighteenth century. And Old Norse gods recur in the Anglo-Saxon epic *Beowulf*. But whether similar connections can be found on the purely linguistic level is a controversial and perhaps even doubtful proposition.

For Clarke, the past was so very much present. Witnessing the opulent celebratory feasts in Norway, he was reminded of the festivals of the Goths, "when animals were roasted whole, and the guests were served with heaps of flesh by attendants in complete armour, who carved with their swords: and they serve also to remind us of those fables of the Edda, or ancient Icelandic Mythology, in which to eat voraciously is described as a qualification, worthy not only of a warrior, but of a God." Clarke reinterpreted the long Scandinavian winter as a season of celebrations and social pleasures. The good cheer displayed by Norwegians made their high streets into a "crowded promenade, more interesting and amusing than that of Hyde Park in London, or the Corso at Rome."

Clarke was ahead of his time in drawing connections between the stone remnants and burial mounds of past civilizations in his home country and those in Scandinavia. "Like the Pyramids of Egypt, they have outlived the memory of the people by whom they were raised," he enthused. "In every country where they are found, the traditions concerning them refer to fabulous ages, and generally to a race of giants." About the knives, axes, and arrowheads he saw in a museum in Trondheim, he wrote, "It is difficult to believe they were not the work of the same people, whether found in Britain, Greenland, or North America." This was not as far-fetched as it may initially seem—there are commonalities between the Indigenous peoples of the Arctic, although they wouldn't be comprehensively studied until the twentieth century by cultural anthropologists such as the American Alfred Irving Hallowell with his 1926 landmark study *Bear Ceremonialism in the Northern Hemisphere*. While Clarke never visited Greenland or North America, he had no scruples about drawing comparisons involving both places, particularly concerning what he saw as their early stage of development. "The only region with which Sweden can properly be compared, is North America, a land of wood and iron, with very few inhabitants, and out of whose hills thou mayest dig brass, but, like America, it is also, as to society, in a state of infancy," he wrote. "It has produced a Linnaeus, because natural history is almost the only study to which the visible objects of such a region can be referred: and almost all its men of letters are still natural historians or chemists. Centuries may elapse before Sweden will produce a Locke."

Even if Clarke was guided by romantic and naive notions, he unequivocally rejected the idea that Scandinavia was the cradle of civilization, the primeval homeland of the Goths and the point of origin of Britons. Instead, he considered Britons and Scandinavians cousins "from one common stock."

Shortly before the turn of the nineteenth century, Giuseppe Acerbi set off from Lombardy for the North. Why did he, a man of the South, "a native of Italy, a country abounding in all the beauties of nature, and the finest productions of art, voluntarily undergo the danger and fatigue of visiting the regions of the Arctic Circle?" His answer to his own question: "There is no people so advanced in civilization, or so highly cultivated, who may not be able to derive some advantage from being acquainted with arts and sciences of other nations, even of such as are the most barbarous." As it had been for his countryman Francesco Negri, whose travelogue Acerbi may well have read, the ultimate destination of this voyage was the North Cape. Acerbi wrote: "Here everything is solitary, everything is sterile, everything sad and despondent. The shadowy forest no longer adorns the brow of the mountain; the singing of the birds, which enlivened even the woods of Lapland, is no longer heard in this scene of desolation; the ruggedness of the dark grey rock is not covered by a single shrub; the only music is the hoarse murmuring of the waves, ever and anon renewing their assaults on the huge masses that oppose them."

In fact, there were few documented travelers from the southern latitudes at the time. Officer and revolutionary Francisco de Miranda, from Caracas (in what is now Venezuela, back then a province of the Spanish Empire), is one exception. He traveled to Scandinavia in 1787 as part of a larger trip across Europe. When he arrived in Stockholm, he had a letter of recommendation from Catherine the Great and got invited to the palace for an audience with King Gustav III. The Spanish ambassador in Stockholm at the time wanted Miranda deported, not knowing that he had already left. Miranda is also rumored to have had an affair with the wife of a wealthy Gothenburg merchant.

Scandinavia was the least risky way for explorers to get to the higher latitudes. The full power of nature was far more perilous in the Arctic, which required another level of preparation and equipment—and far more daring. Prior to the twentieth century, hardly anyone made their way there as private citizens. Among the few who did was Karl Ludwig Giesecke (born Johann Georg Metzler) from Augsburg, Bavaria, who hardly enjoyed a clear-cut scholarly career. He spent years as an actor before translating Mozart's *Le nozze di Figaro* and *Così fan tutte* into German, and later claimed to have authored the libretto of *The Magic Flute*. Lectures by the German naturalist and race theorist Johann Friedrich Blumenbach seem to have inspired him to go into the mineral trade. After providing several European museums with mineralogical collections, he was commissioned by the Royal Greenland Trading Department to research Greenland's varieties of rock. Since Napoleon's armies had destroyed Denmark's fleet of whaling and trading ships, Giesecke was forced to set off for his destination in an English vessel.

Giesecke remained in Greenland from 1806 to 1813, during which time he kept an astonishingly comprehensive diary with the rather specific-sounding title *Mineralogical Travel Journal*. During the summer months, he visited Greenland's western coast and its trading and missionary outposts. Those who had previously traveled to Greenland, whether whalers or proselytes, had stressed the harshness of the climate and the horrors they associated with the island. Although Giesecke was forced to deal with difficult situations and had repeated cause to complain about the unreliability of his assistants in Greenland, over the course of his journey he came to appreciate the fearsome natural beauty there.

For instance, in May 1809, he wrote:

> The sight of this terrible sea of ice with all its glimmering, smooth-as-glass cliffs and its unpredictable fissures and troughs—the sight in all directions, as far as the eye can see into the land, of frozen, dead nature, where no living thing, neither bird nor insect nor worm, is visible, and the uncanny silence is broken only by the beating of the angry waves, the creaking of the snow and the thunder or an iceberg breaking off—entrances the traveler in speechless amazement and makes as vivid an impression on his alert senses as the most charming region of Italy. There the eternal joy and here the eternal sadness of nature! . . . And yet, the indescribably lovely, gigantic grottos, which the combined force of the sun and the sea carved into the coast in the form of now sapphire blue, now emerald green and now silver, crystalline cliffs of ice, though they may collapse in ruins in an instant, fill the soul with a certain anxious joy.

At one in the morning on August 16, 1813, Giesecke boarded the brig *Hvalfisken* to sail back to Europe. "It is truly difficult for me to leave a land that has cordially accommodated me over so many years and to part from friends and acquaintances with whom I fraternally shared many bitter hours and gloomy sights in the past year," he wrote as he departed the planet's largest island. Shortly after his arrival, he was made a professor of mineralogy in Dublin and even given an aristocratic title. He never returned to Germany.

Journeying to Scotland, as to Scandinavia, didn't present foreign visitors with a particularly stern test of courage. There, too, it was easier for women to travel than in the South or in the Middle East, particularly on their own. Emilie von Berlepsch, who visited in 1799, was a close acquaintance of Herder and, as she proudly described herself, "the first German woman who traveled to the fatherland of the bard [Ossian]." Having set off from Hamburg, she made landfall near Glasgow on the "classical ground of Ossian's songs." She arrived with the Scottish scholar James Macdonald, with whom she had corresponded intensively and who had encouraged her to make the trip. Readers of the travelogue *Caledonia* (1802–1804) who followed Berlepsch's footsteps through the dramatic Scottish landscape got to know her as an open, occasionally somewhat naive person engaged in a continual, lively dialogue with herself. She believed that bagpipe music, which had "quite unpleasantly assaulted" her ears, must be a recent distortion of Scandinavian culture: "It is impossible to conceive of the beautiful, gentle emotions of Ossian arising during and being accompanied by this shrill bleating."

Berlepsch was very susceptible to external impressions such as the shift from clear weather to fog and mist: "The sudden transitions and contrasts one encounter in the Highlands are indescribable. In a couple of hours, the whole character of an area can change three or four times so that one feels as though one has been taken from one end of Europe to the other." Bowled over by the historical depths she thought she was witnessing, Berlepsch's experience of Scotland inspired a whole series of complaints about her own homeland: "Why is the German soil so silent? Why do we have no monuments, no echoes of earlier times, no narrative popular song? Certainly, much that was great and good, tragic and tender, took place on German soil, but except in southern Germany, where one can still find some interesting ruins, one can travel from one place to another without being reminded of images from the past and being captivated by them."

It was no accident that Berlepsch traveled to Great Britain. The mood in German-speaking Europe had been pro-British for quite some time, and the intellectual affinities between the two regions stretched back to the Reformation. In the eighteenth century, France may have been culturally predominant, but England, with its liberal-democratic political system, was the role model Germans hoped to emulate, as did French democrats like Voltaire and Montesquieu. By the nineteenth century, London was not just the "workshop of the world," but also, alongside Paris, Europe's most important cultural center. A variety of factors thus encouraged close connections between England and Germany.

Writer Johanna Schopenhauer, the mother of author Adele Schopenhauer and her philosopher brother Arthur, also paid a visit to the north of the British Isles around the turn of the nineteenth century. Years later, she described her experiences in *Travels through England and Scotland*, published in 1818, recalling one extraordinary encounter in particular:

An old man in national garb was sitting on a stone near the churchyard. His long, snow-white beard fluttered in the wind, he looked wild, and a pair of dark eyes glowered from under his high, bald forehead. Plaid was draped vividly over his shoulders like an overcoat, and between his knees he held a small harp from which he violently plucked out disconnected chords. In a powerful deep voice, he sang old popular songs in Scottish Gaelic. His singing was monotonous in tone, more declamation than singing. The entire village had congregated around him, among them a fellow who was one hundred years old. Everyone listened solemnly. We were told that the old man was an itinerant singer, who traveled the countryside, with no home of his own, but welcome wherever he went, like the bards of old. Unfortunately, we were unable to speak with him because he understood no English.

In the summer of 1794, English author and women's rights activist Mary Wollstonecraft made a journey through southern Norway, western Sweden, Denmark, and northern Germany with her 1-year-old daughter Fanny and her governess. This was hardly a vacation trip. Wollstonecraft was there on a mission. With England and France at war, she was trying to help the American businessman Gilbert Imlay, who had attempted to smuggle a large amount of silver from France to Scandinavia. Wollstonecraft wanted to find a ship and retrieve the cargo. It is also known that she was in an unhappy relationship with Imlay, who was Fanny's father. Three weeks prior to the trip she had attempted suicide, because Imlay was involved with another woman. Of course, nothing of this business or personal background is mentioned in her book.

In Scandinavia, Wollstonecraft allegedly met lots of people and patiently answered their questions: "As the Norwegians do not frequently see travelers, they are very curious to know their business, and who they are—so curious, that I was half tempted to adopt Dr. Franklin's plan, when travelling in America, where they are equally prying, which was to write on a paper, for public inspection, my name, from whence I came, where I was going, and what was my business. . . . A woman coming alone interested them. And I know not whether my weariness gave me a look of peculiar delicacy, but they approached to assist me, and inquire after my wants, as if they were afraid to hurt, and wished to protect me" (from *Letters Written during a Short Residence in Sweden, Norway, and Denmark*).

In her correspondence, Wollstonecraft wrote of how deeply impressed she was by natural phenomena, especially when midnight—or, as she called it, the "noon of night"—approached. She stayed awake though the night, a night "such as I had never before seen or felt. . . . The very air was balmy as it freshened into morn, producing the most voluptuous sensations. A vague pleasurable sentiment absorbed me, as I opened my bosom to the embraces of nature; and my soul rose to its Author, with the chirping of the solitary birds, which began to feel, rather than see, advancing day. I had leisure to mark its progress." However, she wasn't lucky enough to catch a glimpse of a bear in the wild, most likely because she only traveled developed areas of Scandinavia. Wollstonecraft became convinced that the first human inhabitants of Earth must have been at home in the North because only there would they have had the chance to pray to the sun, which was so seldom seen: "Man must therefore have been placed in the north, to tempt him to run after the sun, in order that the different parts of the earth might be peopled. Nor do I wonder that hordes of barbarians always poured out of these regions to seek for milder climes, when nothing like cultivation attached them to the soil."

Wollstonecraft sought to characterize the mentality of various types of Scandinavians in succinct terms, writing, "The Norwegians appear to me a sensible, shrewd people, with little scientific knowledge, and still less taste for literature; but they are arriving at the epoch which precedes the introduction of the arts and sciences." In another passage, she called Norway "the most free community I have ever observed. . . . I never yet have heard of anything like domineering or oppression, excepting such as has arisen from natural causes. The freedom the people enjoy may, perhaps, render them a little litigious, and subject them to the impositions of cunning practitioners of the law; but the authority of office is bounded, and the emoluments of it do not destroy its utility." Further to the south, she remarked upon Danish conservatism, as many people at the time did: "The Danes, in general, seem extremely averse to innovation, and if happiness only consists in opinion, they are the happiest people in the world; for I never saw any so well satisfied with their own situation. Yet the climate appears to be very disagreeable, the weather being dry and sultry, or moist and cold; the atmosphere never having that sharp, bracing purity, which in Norway prepares you to brave its rigours. I do not hear the inhabitants of this place talk with delight of the winter, which is the constant theme of the Norwegians; on the contrary, they seem to dread its comfortless inclemency."

Her report, which is in the genre of the sentimental journey (the most famous at the time was Laurence Sterne's book on his travels in France and Italy), is not without its contradictions. "Though I do not speak Danish, I knew that I could see a great deal: yes, I am persuaded that I have formed a very just opionion of the character of the Norwegians, without being able to hold converse with them," she wrote. It could be asked how she arrived at her bold generalizations.

Denmark long had a special status in Europe as Germany's direct neighbor. Although Danish was closely related linguistically to Swedish and Norwegian, culturally the country had had a heavy German influence, before it began to focus more on Great Britain. In those days, Denmark's borders stretched down to the Elbe River near Hamburg. Altona—now a district of that northern German city—was the second largest Danish metropolis in the nineteenth century after Copenhagen. Local resistance to the Danish Crown grew throughout the century, though, and in 1863, Prussian troops seized the city and the northern regions of Schleswig and Holstein in what is commonly regarded as the first act in creating a unified German nation-state.

What struck German writer Johann Gottfried Seume most about the town of Fagerhult, in southern Sweden, during his 1805 trip were the trees, particularly the beeches: "I suddenly saw this region here in such perfection and beauty as can rarely be observed in the Thuringian Forest or on Lago Albano." But although he drew a comparison with Germany's national tree, the oak, he refrained from constructing any broad cultural affinities between Germany and Scandinavia. Seume's travels took him via Poland to Russia, where he had previously served as lieutenant in the military for more than ten years, then on to Finland and from there to Sweden and Denmark.

He made it as far as Stockholm, the "paradise of the North." There, his recollections of a journey to Italy made three years prior remained fresh: "Stockholm is one of the most delightful places I've ever seen. If Lake Malar [now called Mälaren] had the sun of Lago d'Arno [a lake in Lombardy, northern Italy], it would be closer to Elysium than Florence is." In Uppsala, this former theology student got a look at the *Codex Argenteus* manuscript, the fourth-century Ulfilas translation of the Bible into Gothic, written in silver and gold letters on purple parchment. In Stockholm's old town, he visited the burial mounds of the heathen kings and the megalith graves of northern Germany. Traveling south, he noted that "wild strata of granite" alternated with picturesque little idylls. At the end of his trip he wrote: "Sweden is probably the most humane and friendly country in the North. Despite all the poverty which can be neither denied nor concealed, everywhere you go there is an orderliness and an appearance of prosperity, in which everything is comfortable in patriarchal security."

But not all visitors found Scandinavia to be a dream location, as is evident in Jean-Jacques Ampère's (the son of the famous physicist André-Marie Ampère) 1833 travelogue bursting with observations and comments on literature that was "dedicated to the North, to Germany and Scandinavia." Upon arriving in Sweden, he wrote: "The first faces I could make out were those of three sailors, whose blond hair, light eyes, white skin, powerful builds, calm movements as though they were one being and implacable ease provided an astonishing example of the Scandinavian type." Unlike in southern Europe, life in the cities took place inside. Walking the streets of Malmö, Ampère encountered only wagoners and sailors. From Copenhagen, which he had difficulty summing up, he traveled by steamboat via Gothenburg and Trollhättan to Norway, a land without an aristocracy, where "citizens were completely equal." But otherwise, Ampère's account was carping: "It's regrettable that at the end of one of these valleys, one was not confronted with my Montblanc, to which they would fit better than the shabby valley of Chamonix. There is no denying that the North with its extended forests, its great lakes, its long rivers and its large number of cliffs suffers from the fact that it is towered over by massive mountain peaks crowning this harmonious immensity." The Dovrefjell, at the heart of Norway, was for Ampère the St. Gotthard Pass [the pass connecting northern and southern Switzerland] of the Scandinavian Alps, a place where he felt himself entirely "in the presence of Ossian" (all quotes from *Littératures et Voyages: Allemagne et Scandinavie*).

When he caught a glimpse of the "depressing ocean of the North," he felt lost, as though he were in one of the uninhabited extremities of the world. Sadness is a running theme in Ampère's extensive portrait as the "essential characteristic of the North," one that could be found in the "calm and the immensity of nature, in the hopeless eyes of its people and its slow gait and mournful songs, in the fogs rolling in off the ocean, in its long nights and sundowns." Ampère repeatedly conjured up images he recalled from the South, a coastal scene in Napoli full of happily shrieking people, for instance. Perhaps it was his way of sharpening the contrast, or maybe it just made his situation more tolerable for a while. In Lapland, he grew even more unhappy, perceiving the landscape as positively hostile and "the ugliest thing in the universe." As lonely as he felt there, he had no idea where he could journey on to.

France, Ampère's homeland, featured a unique comingling of southern and northern influences, with northern and Romance culture confronting—or perhaps complementing—one another. Views on the North in France were similar to those in Germany and Great Britain. There, too, the eighteenth century experienced a rampant Celtophilia, in which languages, names, and architecture were traced back to supposedly Celtic origins. It was even proposed that Celtic was the primeval human language. Breton played a central role as a Celtic tongue, which was reinterpreted as the successor to Gallic. In his 1783 *Origines Gauloises*, Théophile Malo Corret de la Tour d'Auvergne was one of the most important proponents of this idea. The movement gained additional momentum with Henri Martin's 1834 *Histoire de France*. He posited a deep, mystical connection with the past that would become key to French national identity, writing of "our ancestors the Gauls," the historic group of Celtic peoples in Continental Europe.

As strongly as French intellectuals continued to orient themselves toward the classical literary tradition, they also developed a strong connection to Scandinavia. The most famous figure in this context was Anne Louise Germaine Necker, better known as Madame de Staël. Born in Paris, she was raised by her Swiss Protestant parents and then married the Swedish diplomat Baron Erik Magnus Staël von Holstein, prompting her early affinity with Scandinavia. Their wedding was preceded by years of negotiation at the highest level between France and Sweden—the union was explicitly designed to improve relations between the two countries.

Madame de Staël's role as a cultural mediator between southern and northern Europe in the late-eighteenth and early-nineteenth centuries was thus predetermined. Thanks to her repeated travels and long spells outside France, she continued to develop her unconventional views, collecting enemies with her praise of northern literature. She not only included but stressed German and Danish letters. She regarded southern literature—in Greek, Latin, Italian, Spanish, and French—as part of the Homeric tradition, assigning Ossian the role of the "Homer of the North" and holding up the Old Norse writing as high culture. This amounted to an intellectual revolution for her compatriots. For de Staël, French literature was no longer the universal standard, and she demanded that French audiences no longer focus exclusively on classical antiquity, but also—and indeed primarily—on the traditions of the North.

When East Was North

The before-mentioned Swedish ecclesiastic Catholic Olaus Magnus, creator of the *Carta marina*, an imaginatively illustrated map of northern Europe accompanied by a detailed commentary, considered Russians one of the *gentes septentrionales*, peoples of the North. This was the general European view during the Middle Ages and early modern era. Magnus's map depicts Swedish soldiers armed with crossbows and Russians carrying simple bows and arrows firing at one another. Relations between Sweden and Russia were in fact very tense. By the time Magnus finished his map in 1539, the Treaty of Novgorod, which established a truce between the Grand Duchy of Moscow and Sweden, was only 2 years old. It didn't hold for long. By 1554, the two sides were back at war.

Magnus himself never made it near Moscow or the surrounding area, but he did spend time in Gdansk. At the time, Gdansk was not only a major trading center, but also a magnet for Baltic intellectuals. In his most comprehensive work, *A Description of the Northern Peoples*, published in Rome in 1555, Magnus describes fishing and hunting for pelts as characteristic of Russia and mentions the merchants' habit of using counterfeit coins, hinting at their supposed dishonesty in business matters. Russians, he furthermore noted, wore the so-called *kalpak*, a high-crowned cap made of felt. Magnus also described the Grand Duke of Moscow bearing a sword that symbolized the *furor barbaricus* (barbarian fury). The illustrations in Magnus's book were equally martial, including a depiction of Russian pirates, although there are also images of a meeting between representatives of various countries, seemingly at the Moscow court, as evidence that relations between Scandinavians and Muscovites weren't invariably hostile. Nonetheless, due to differences in mentality, mores, and confession (Russia was Greek Orthodox, Sweden Roman Catholic), Moscow was the part of the North that remained most alien to Magnus and his compatriots.

In general, Russia long remained terra incognita—a "distant northern empire"—for Western travelers. Whereas visitors from western and central Europe could make themselves understood to a degree in Scandinavia, their inability in the Slavic languages presented far greater problems in Russia if they didn't have interpreters with them or had no contact with German speakers in Russian cities. The confessional chasm between the Protestant and the Russian Orthodox churches also didn't exactly lead to mutual understanding. Russia was perceived not just as foreign and unknown, but positively antithetical to the West and South. And many people asked themselves: what of interest could be seen there anyway?

At the time, Peter the Great was known in Europe as both the "lord of the entire northern land" and the "Turk of the North," the implication of the latter being that one day the Russian Empire might become as dangerous as the Ottoman Empire had been. Peter traveled to Prussia, Holland, and England, met with shipbuilders, and attempted to reform and modernize the Russian economic and educational system by recruiting specialists from western Europe. The military was instructed to cut their beards and adopt western-style clothing. St. Petersburg was founded in 1703, with official buildings modeled after those in the great western European capitals.

When Swedes captured in the Great Northern War (1700–1721) were sent to Siberia, they recorded their experiences in writing, relaying information about these faraway territories to Europe. The conflict put the Kingdom of Sweden against a coalition of the Russian Empire, Saxony-Pologne, and Norway-Denmark for dominance of the Baltic region. When the war ended, Sweden lost its status as a major European power, and the Russian Empire grew stronger. Among those captured by the Russians was Philipp Johann von Strahlenberg, a Swedish officer and geographer of German origin, who was taken prisoner in 1709 and returned to Stockholm as late as 1722. He wrote a report of his experiences, in which he described, among other things, the languages of the various central Asian peoples and Indigenous Siberians. It was translated into German, French, English, and Spanish. Strahlenberg is also famous for relocating the dividing line between Europe and Asia to the Ural Mountains.

When Catherine the Great came to power in 1762, she soon brought western European scientists and intellectuals to St. Petersburg and commissioned the city's art collections, its natural history museum, the Winter Palace, and the Admiralty Building. Soon these were featured in travelogues, sparking European interest in St. Petersburg, Moscow, and the Baltic states. From then on, the so-called northern tour, encompassing both Scandinavia and Russia, gained popularity among British travelers. Catherine the Great, whom Voltaire once called the "Semiramis of the North" (after a mythological queen of Babylon) and who was also known as the "northern Minerva," was empress until 1796 and thus the country's longest-ruling female leader.

Located in the same remote high latitudes as northern Canada and Alaska, with its almost endless expanse of tundra and taiga, Siberia was different. Its status as part of the North was never questioned, and at least to western eyes, it remained *terra incognita* until about four hundred years ago. That began to change as the result of the Great Northern Expedition, which was conceived by Peter the Great and implemented by Empresses Anna and Elizabeth. Led by Vitus Bering, a Dane working on behalf of Russia, it was carried out from 1733 to 1743 with the goal of exploring the eastern reaches of Siberia. Together with the Russian Aleksei Chirikov, Bering discovered the Aleutian Islands in 1841 and also reached Alaska. Peter Simon Pallas, a zoologist and botanist of Prussian origin who spent his working life in Russia, later continued in this vein of Siberian exploration, writing a two-thousand-page book called *Travels through the Various Provinces of the Russian Empire* (1771). It made him famous well beyond the borders of Russia and triggered further interest in this vast, remote region that today is often associated with prisons, oppression, the thawing of permafrost, and, more recently, intense wildfires.

Later travelogues were not exactly apt to awaken Europeans' desire to travel to this difficult-to-reach part of the planet. On the contrary, Westerners' experiences often only confirmed and reinforced their countrymen's skepticism and prejudices. For instance, in 1800, German author August von Kotzebue was arrested at the Russian border on suspicion of being an anti-royalist Jacobin and sent to Tobolsk and Kurgan in southwestern Siberia, where he was kept for more than a year before being released. In his book *The Strangest Year of My Life*, he wrote: "My favorite thing to do was to wander around under the open skies. If only the intolerable heat and the even more intolerable flies in the evening had allowed this more often. Not a day went by when the thermometer didn't get above 26 to 28 on the Réaumur scale [90.5°–95°F], and there were at least four, five or sometimes six thunderstorms that brewed up and clashed from all directions, often bringing heavy rains that nonetheless didn't cool the air." Still, Kotzebue did have some words of praise for the rough climate, which he considered salubrious: "My doctor knew of only two main illnesses and two that could be easily avoided. One was syphilis, and the other was cold fever common because of the rapid change in air temperature after sundown. Chastity and warm clothing to wrap up in at night are all one needs in Siberia to reach a healthy, advanced age."

These were hardly the most persuasive arguments to visit a place so far away. Kotzebue himself almost died in an accident with a horse-drawn wagon in Kungur. As great a portion of the Northern Hemisphere as Siberia may have occupied—almost 10 percent of Earth's landmass—travelers didn't associate it with much that was positive. Conditions there were simply too hostile.

German-Baltic doctor Alexander Theodor von Middendorff visited Lapland in 1840, and shortly thereafter, commissioned by Russia, he undertook an expedition to the extreme north of Siberia, where, as a physician, he seems to have been able to gain the trust of the people who lived in this inhospitable region—whether they were Russian settlers or members of the Indigenous population. The journey was a real test. Middendorff struggled through the rough terrain of the tundra, his eyes dazzled by mirages, and battled the riptides of the Sea of Okhotsk and the snows of the Kolyma Upland. Humanity is indebted to him for a wealth of information about Siberia's Indigenous people, plants, animals, geographical and morphological construction, climate, soil, and tree lines, all of which went into his voluminous *Travels to the Extreme North and East of Siberia* (1847–1875).

A few decades later, in 1891, the English nurse, missionary, and adventurer Kate Marsden embarked on a most unlikely expedition to northeastern Siberia. She had already taken part in a mission to treat Russian casualties in the Russo-Turkish war in Bulgaria and had traveled to New Zealand to help her tuberculosis-ridden sister and assist in running a hospital and training nurses. The harsh living conditions she encountered on her journey to the Extreme North are documented in her 1893 book *On sledge and Horseback to Outcast Siberian Lepers:* "Sometimes we came to a large lake, which we had to glide over, meeting, now and then, a few men, who had cut holes in the lake, and were lying on the ice, fishing. Russian peasants sit and recline on blocks of ice, as if Primitive Dwellings. . . . The cold of Russia has one decided effect: it finds out the weakest young people, and kills them off before they reach manhood or womanhood; so that weak and delicate men and women are seldom met with, at least, in country districts."

Marsden's goal was to examine Siberian lepers and find a cure for the disease, hoping to use an unspecified medicinal herb: "I was also told that the herb was to be found in the far-off Yakutsk province of Siberia, where there were many lepers; but, being so jealously kept a secret by the natives, no one who wished to make experiments with it from mercenary motives could hope to obtain any information."

While her hope of finding an herbal remedy for the disease in this "vast wild Siberia" came to naught, Marsden did raise considerable money for a leprosy hospital, which opened in Vilyusk in 1897. Having garnered attention for her endeavors, she received audiences with Queen Victoria, the Princess of Wales, and Russian Empress Maria Feodorovna. In 1892, Marsden became one of the first female fellows of the Royal Geographical Society. Nonetheless, she was confronted with campaigns trying to discredit her with accusations that she had misused the funds she had raised for her own benefit, that she was a political spy, that she had fabricated parts of the story of her Siberian journey, and that she was a lesbian.

Climate Makes the Man

Do northern people lack passion? Is there a connection between their toughness and the harshness of the landscape or the winds coming from there? Speculations about how climatic conditions affected people's physical constitution began in antiquity and can be found across the ages. Seneca described Boreas as a "terrible north wind," while Ovid called Auster, a scirocco, the "death-bringing south wind." A passage from the enormously popular polemic *The Weeks* by the sixteenth-century Huguenot writer Guillaume de Saluste Du Bartas reads:

> *The northern-man is fair, the southern foul:*
> *That's white, this black; that smiles and this doth scoul;*
> *Th'one blithe & frolike, th'other dull & froward;*
> *Th'one's full of courage, th'other fearfull coward;*
> *Th'one's hair is harsh, big, curled, th'others slender;*

Th'one loveth labour, th'other books doth tender;
Th'one's hot and moist, the other's hot and dry.

Montesquieu would later adopt these ideas, albeit in more differentiated fashion. He used the contrast between a cold cultural zone and a hot one as the basis for a cultural anthropology that privileged the man of the North, insofar as he remained on his home terrain, over the man of the extreme South. Crucially, Montesquieu disputed that there were any inherently northern or southern character traits, insisting instead that people were formed by their surrounding climate. In his 1748 essay "Of Laws in Relation to the Nature of the Climate," he conflated climate and mentality in idiosyncratic fashion: "The inhabitants of warm countries are, like old men, timorous; the people in cold countries are, like young men, brave. If we reflect on the late wars . . . we shall find that the northern people, transplanted into southern regions, did not perform such exploits as their countrymen who, fighting in their own climate, possessed their full vigor and courage." He also held that freedom, such as it existed in Europe, originated with the Scandinavian peoples, whereas he associated the South and the Orient with a distorted picture of despotism he believed still predominated there. This was Montesquieu's justification for a fundamentally altered view of northern Europe.

A few years later, in his lectures on physical geography, the German philosopher Immanuel Kant assigned humanity to various "races" with differing characters. He proposed: "If one enquires as to the sources of the forms and temperament inherent in a people, then one need only consider the variations of animals in relation of form and behavior, for as soon as they are transported to a different climate, different air and food, etc., make them to be different from their descendants. A squirrel that is brown here will become grey in Siberia. A European dog taken to Guinea will become misshapen and bald, and so will its descendants." Kant expanded this logic to human beings: "The descendants of the northern peoples who went to Spain not only have bodies that are not nearly as strong as they were originally, but also their temperament has changed into one very different from that of a Norwegian or Dane. The inhabitant of the temperate zone, especially in its central part, is more beautiful in body, harder working, more witty, more moderate in his passions, and more sensible than any other kind of people in the world. Consequently, these people have always taught the rest [of the world] and vanquished them by the use of weapons. The Romans, Greeks, the ancient Nordic peoples, Genghis Khan, the Turks, Tamburlaine, and the Europeans after Columbus's discoveries, have astounded all the southern countries with their arts and their weapons."

Kant suggests a familiarity with circumstances in faraway places, which is ironic, because he spent nearly all his life in Königsberg (today, the Russian exclave of Kaliningrad), in provincial East Prussia, and received much of his knowledge from often obscure travel accounts and from conversing with sailors at the harbor of his home city.

Shot Through with
Gods and Demons

Once the Old Norse writings had been deciphered, scholars soon made the attempt to reconstruct the worldview of the "Germanic" tribes. Central to this project was Wilhelm Grimm, one of the famous Brothers Grimm, who compiled his volume of *Old Danish Heroic Songs, Ballads and Fairy Tales* in 1811. Grimm also studied German, English, and Scandinavian runes, concluding in his 1821 book *On German Runes* that "the sixteen Old Norse runes were the basis of the English and German ones. Gustav Thormod Legis (a pseudonym for Anton Thormond Glückselig), a German-language scholar who lived in Prague, built upon Grimm's work in his 1829 *Treasure Trove of the Old North*. "The unity of the German and Scandinavian lineage remains beyond doubt for now and all time," he asserted, postulating that "the German and Scandinavian spirit is completely identical in the religious and political sense."

Wilhelm Grimm's brother Jakob followed with his three-volume *German Mythology* in 1835. Using everything from fairy tales to recorded customs and Old Norse writings, he came up with a reconstructed Germanic mythology, which until then had been considered a *terra incognita* overshadowed by the preserved myths of Scandinavia. Jakob Grimm was convinced that "the hearts [of the Germanic tribes] were full of faith in God and gods, that cheerful and grand, if incomplete notions of higher beings, the triumph of victory and contempt for death invigorated and elevated their lives and that their nature and disposition had nothing of that dully brooding prostration before idols and monoliths which has been mislabeled as fetishism." The results of his work fulfilled all his expectations: "Greater than the deviations is the concordance, and Germany, which converted to Christianity and became educated earlier, can pay back the far richer north for the invaluable information about how the ruins of its myths fit together by providing older historical witnesses for more recent written records."

Today there is a highly romanticized image of the Brothers Grimm traveling from village to village, listening to the people and assiduously collecting old stories in an attempt to satisfy people's desire for a fairy-tale reality. One of the Grimms' great achievements was to popularize a series of tales that were previously only passed on orally, including "Cinderella," "Hansel and Gretel," "Rumpelstiltskin," "Sleeping Beauty" and "Snow White"—all of which remain canonical today, thanks in part to the film adaptations by the Walt Disney Studios. But the latest research has uncovered a darker side to their work, including a number of stigmatizing, anti-Semitic statements that are no less dangerous for being diffusely formulated. On one occasion, for instance, the brothers speak of "Jewish impertinence and pushiness." Their collections elevated narratives like "The Wandering Jew," "The Girl Who Was Killed by Jews," and "The Jews' Stones," which were full of anti-Jewish clichés and ritual murder legends, into collective German culture as putative examples of popular genius. Precisely because their work was so well known, the Grimms played a not inconsiderable role in making opposition to Jewish assimilation acceptable in polite society. This is all the more surprising because we know that the brothers maintained social contacts with Jews, such as a tutor named Jochil, who gave Jakob his first Hebrew lessons, and the banker Carl Rothschild.

We can assume that the Grimms were particularly revered among many readers who resented Jews but didn't always clearly express those feelings. For many such people, the Grimms' orientation toward the North also meant turning their backs on the Judeo-Christian past. It was an act of rebellion tracing itself back to unclear roots and creating a dubious collective mythology. In the Romantic epoch and later, the search for German national identity was often fatefully connected with anti-Jewish resentment, which had existed for centuries and was accompanied by severe restrictions on Jews' civil rights in the German states. These limitations on advancement in society played an important part in the great wave of German Jews emigrating to the United States in the nineteenth century.

Fascinated by superstitions and popular stories, German poet Heinrich Heine submerged himself in the world of fairy-tale beings, in particular elves, of which he found numerous examples in Danish folk songs and Gaelic sagas. Heine, born into a Jewish family and often at odds with German authorities for his political stance, had a more playful approach to the motifs of North and South, one that undercut a strict dualism. Immune to any chauvinist Germanophile worship of the North, he took elements from Norse mythology to form mysterious but never leaden or cultish scenes. From the Old Norse writings, Heine adapted kobolds, Valkyries, and even the Norns, "the Parcae of the North,"—women dressed in swan feathers who determined the fates of human beings and with which he was particularly struck (he mentioned them in his 1837 *Elementary Spirits).*

In *Book of Songs*, Heine posited an enchanting connection between the two points on the compass:

A pine-tree's standing lonely
In the North on a mountain's brow,

Nodding with whitest cover,
Wrapped up by the ice and snow.
He's dreaming of a palm-tree,
Which, far in the Morning Land,
Lonely and silent sorrows
Mid burning rocks and sand.

While in Germany Old Norse writings served as a catalyst for feelings of Germanic identity, attitudes in Scandinavia were more relaxed and less full of pathos. Scandinavians were often skeptical about the German appropriation of their ancient traditions, occasionally viewing it as an insult to their national pride. Many people rejected being lumped into a single Scandinavian North. Even if, with the exception of Finnish, the Scandinavian languages were all closely related, with the formation of the Scandinavian nation-states they nonetheless represented five separate official tongues and carried significant cultural differences. In the realm of fine art, there were arguments about how the protagonists of Norse mythology could be convincingly depicted and whether Greek forms should be adapted to that end. Swedish author Erik Gustaf Geijer, for instance, categorically refused to depict the one-eyed Odin realistically. In general, the Norse gods were considered insufficiently "aesthetic."

The conservative Swedish nationalist Jacob August von Hartmannsdorff invoked the Germanic tribes' mutual strength in "resisting the Slavs and Gauls." Yet such expressions of pan-Germanism remained the exception. Scandinavians were content with their own peoples and skeptical and disinclined toward the idea of a great Germanic alliance of states. The Norwegian literary scholar Sophus Bugge advanced the thesis in the late nineteenth century that the songs of the *Edda* and the Icelandic Sagas originated in the Christian-Roman tradition and came to Scandinavia via England. But this was very much a fringe view.

Alongside the Old Norse writings and Grimm's pastiche of German stories, there was an epic from the Finnish North. Published in 1835, The

Kalevala or Old Runes of Karelia concerning the Ancient Times of the Finnish People was based on a compilation of songs from the oral tradition by Elias Lönnrot, who had traveled to the Karelian region of eastern Finland, written down the songs of the so-called rune singers, and combined them into a cohesive narrative, using his imagination to fill in the gaps. None of it can be proved to be "ancient," because it's Lönnrot's artistic composition, but still, the *Kalevala* is composed of 97 percent collected material, with Lönnrot writing only 3 percent himself. According to the myth of creation in this work, the world emerged from a diving duck's egg.

The *Kalevala* was very important in the creation of a Finnish national identity, since before its publication, the Finns had no written language of their own. February 28, Finland's Independence Day, is also known and celebrated as Kalevala Day.

"To the North Its End Shall Be Cast"

"The Scandinavians are our brothers," Ernst Moritz Arndt once asserted. Arndt, an early-nineteenth-century German nationalist writer, was hopeful that the peoples of the North would help German speakers resist France, the enemy from the West. In 1813, Sweden joined the international alliance against Napoleon, who suffered a crushing defeat at the Battle of Nations outside Leipzig. Later, there were plans to admit Denmark to the nineteenth-century German Confederation. In his 1843 *Essay on the Comparative History of Peoples*, Arndt made an impassioned plea: "Toward the North, it is toward the North we must look. The wise and more noble Danes and Swedes are watching us. They are our born alliance partners thanks to all of the most natural bonds, thanks to geography, education, lineage, religion and a common enemy who lurks on both of our borders and would like to tear the entire Baltic Sea from Germanic hands." He was guided by the principle that people became like their land—an idea that left considerable room for various interpretations. He wrote: "Much here in the North that seems born happy and triumphant remains undeveloped or semi-developed like a clump of substance, rotting away in the fullness of its germs and drives that never finds the necessary sun. In the south, everything finds its natural development easily. In the north, a lot decays because of overabundance that cannot gain proportion and form."

As evenhanded as Arndt sounds here, he thought the halfway point between the Arctic and the equator was the ideal soil for cultural development—not coincidentally, this was where he himself called home! For Arndt, the Germans were the epitome of settledness despite admittedly being, "as Christians, roving pilgrims and foreigners on earth in all respects." The antithesis of Germans, in Arndt's eyes, were "the Jews and gypsies scattered and intimidated across the great world, who never had a place on earth where they had the right to lay their heads."

Obsessed with all things German and preaching a philosophy of northern love of nature, Arndt's world was divided along extremely clear lines: on the one hand the Germanic tribes, on the other the Romans; on the one hand the Germans, on the other the Jews; on the one hand the forest, on the other the desert. He degraded the seminomadic Sámi people as "spoilers of the forest," while on another occasion berating Italy as the "land of lemons and bandits." It certainly couldn't become more cliché ridden than this.

In Arndt's view, the forests were the bond—an all-important criterion—that made Germany and Scandinavia related cultural realms. Arndt accused not only his archenemy France, but also England and the Netherlands, of leveling their forests and replacing them with soulless parks and fields. Conversely, he mourned the "sad evisceration of land and hearts" and praised Sweden as a role model, trying to rouse Germans in a fight for liberty.

Like Arndt, the popular Berlin author Theodor Mügge combined geography and politics. He had surveyed Norway in all its impressive length and had come away enthusiastic. In his 1844 book *Sketches from the North*, he wrote of Norway as the home of "tribally related people, whose language, customs, institutions and way of thinking recall the lives of our forefathers and our own lives at home to the same extent that their newly founded state is built on principals of primeval Germanic freedom." Norway, the besotted Mügge continued, was a "state with an enclosing system, without an aristocracy, a military class, bureaucracy, rank, titles and orders!" It was a country that enjoyed freedom of the press, "in which farmers, too, can read." Mügge was a democratic, liberal-minded author of the *Vormärz* (the period leading up to the revolutions of March 1848), whose praise for Norway could of course be read as tacit criticism of the political circumstances in his own country. To leave readers in no doubt about his sympathies, he included the text of the Norwegian constitution in his travelogue. He was also flattered that during his time in Norway, people often called out to him that Germany was "the heart of the world."

Albrecht von Roon, in his 1845 *Study of Geography, Peoples and States*, was of a similar mind, albeit more interested in geographical, climatological, and cultural aspects. "The Scandinavians are Northerners, sea and mountain people, but always at the same time Germanic people," Roon wrote. In contrast to the British Isles, which were the "jumping off point for Europe and the Germanic world's transoceanic traffic," Scandinavia was the "homeland of the Varangians, the kings of the seas [and] the Vikings" and was oriented toward the "Polar North." This, Roon claimed, had an especially profound effect on people's character: "The stringency of northern nature as well as the limitations imposed by maritime isolation, roughness and indomitability made this influence more powerful still."

But although a number of intellectuals longed for closer ties to Scandinavia, German interest in the North on the whole was modest at this point—especially when compared with the fascination many Germans had with North America ahead of what would be an unprecedented mass emigration there. For example, Karl Simrock—translator of the *Nibelungenlied* and editor of the poetry of twelfth- and thirteen-century German poet Walther von der Vogelweide and an 1851 edition of the *Edda*—wrote: "It's entirely possible that we know nothing and don't want to know anything about the Norse gods because they are our own, since admittedly it is an all-too-German characteristic to root around in every corner of the world—in Rome and Greece, in England and Spain, in Arabia, India and China—running down dead ends and feeling our way around like blind people in their own home." Perhaps it would have been cleverer, Simrock added, to play down the feelings of German-northern connection and to "stay quiet about the identical nature of Norse and Germanic gods."

It wasn't until Richard Wagner that the German appropriation of the North picked up pace. Wagner was the first composer to use Scandinavian subject matter in his operas. His early work *The Flying Dutchman*, from 1843, was composed after he had been dramatically forced to flee Riga to evade creditors. Originally, Wagner set that opera on the Cape of Good Hope before moving it first to Scotland and finally to the coast of Norway. The main sources for Wagner's *Ring of the Nibelungs* were Icelandic, mediated in part though the writer Friedrich de la Motte-Fouqué: the two *Edda*, parts of the *Völsunga Saga*, and material taken from other sagas. Odin became Wotan; Sigurd, Siegfried; and Brynhildr, Brünnhilde.

For a quarter of a century, Wagner worked on four connected operas, which premiered from August 13 to August 17, 1876, to mark the opening of the Bayreuth Festival Theater: *The Ring Cycle* was the story of the twilight of the gods and the appearance of free man. Wagner's goal was to create a *Gesamtkunstwerk*, a "total work of art" combining different art forms, such as music, poetry, and dance, into a symbiosis capable of radiating out into the far reaches of society. The "twilight of the gods" enthralled countless admirers in Germany and beyond. One major source of appeal was Wagner's prophetic quality, embodied in the gesture of casting a rope "to the north," a motif that goes back to the *Edda*. Wagner's Siegfried is a Nordic hero who saves the world, with humanity wandering toward the North. Everything happens under the emblem of light. In the North, Wagner suggests, the world will be "healed."

The Germanophile biologist and philosopher Houston Stewart Chamberlain—who was born in Portsmouth, England, raised in France, and married to Wagner's daughter Eva in 1908—is best known for his 1899 work *The Foundations of the Nineteenth Century*. Obsessed by the

Darwinist idea of using "selective breeding" to eliminate what he considered inferior elements of human society, he was a virulent anti-Semite who saw Jews and Aryans as incompatible, rejecting all notions of assimilation or conversion.

Chamberlain held regular lectures at the Wagner Society in Vienna, and he once remarked that his father-in-law was the "sun of his life," who had helped him experience the "completely developed consciousness of Germany." Chamberlain's opinions were typical of many people who discovered the work of the "master" composer. He also carried on a correspondence of more than two decades with Kaiser Wilhelm II, who was convinced that Christianity had developed from heathen religion and not from Judaism. From exile in the Netherlands after the First World War, Wilhelm wrote: "The Germanic character in its majesty was only made clear and preached to an astonished German people by Chamberlain." It was no accident that Chamberlain would later become a major influence on National Socialism, especially on the chief ideologue, Alfred Rosenberg. In later life, he praised Hitler as a "new Parsifal" and a "savior."

The Dubious Cradle
of Humanity

The model of evolution developed by Charles Darwin increasingly gained traction, bringing about a revolution in scientific thinking. It was now clear that natural and human history were interlinked. What did this mean for how people imagined the North? Had the time come to reevaluate the region's role in prehistory? Could it be that the northern peoples and their cultures had emerged independently from those elsewhere? Was it possible that Europe's original inhabitants were actually Germanic?

Based on the wealth of new knowledge, the idea of a long Germanic prehistory seemed worthy of closer examination. And regardless of whether the origins of the northern cultures were attributed to the North itself or to India or Persia, many researchers now considered belief in the biblical story of creation—scorned by some as "Jewish fables"—to be out of date. No one could imagine what the consequences this shift in thinking would have.

The idea that White people originated in the Caucasus, which in the nineteenth century was closely entwined with the question of the genesis of the Germanic peoples, was first formulated by Johann Friedrich Blumenbach. In 1776, he used the term *Caucasian* to refer to those peoples who were "predominantly white in color" and, in his eyes, most beautiful. Later the writer Joseph Görres also traced the historical roots of the European peoples to the Caucasus. In his 1807 essay "Religion in History," he wrote: "All that is powerfully, ruggedly and jauntily heroic invariably had its epicenter in [the Caucasus]; all great conquerors and all world-commanding characters have poured down from its heights like wild mountain streams, and the earth's other mountains willingly acknowledged this range as their king. Just as in later ages the Celtic and Germanic myths and those of the northern Scandinavians that all spring from the genuine heroic spirit began there." Görres and others suggested that the mysterious origins of the Germanic peoples lay in the mountains connecting the Black and Caspian Seas. Was Noah's ark, as they asked, not stranded after the Flood at Mount Ararat, in the Armenian mountains, not far south of the Caucasus?

During the second half of the eighteenth century, the Old Norse texts and the Ossian saga began to rival Greek and Roman mythology in popularity, at least among some intellectual circles. But despite the discovery and recognition of the storytelling riches of the North, the broad consensus remained that humanity's origins lay in the East. *"Ex oriente lux!"* was the accepted wisdom—light comes from the east! However, as research into prehistorical humankind brought revolutionary advances in knowledge, this and other sacrosanct assumptions were called into question. During the nineteenth century, the study of ancient cultures—at long last also including those of northern and western Europe—shook the foundations of belief in what had long been Christian dogma: that humanity, created by God all at once in the biblical lands of the Near East, had existed for approximately six thousand years. Archbishop James Ussher had come to this conclusion in 1650 based on an analysis of the Old Testament. According to his calculations, the world was created on a very specific date: October 23, 4004 BCE.

Of course, the biblical story of the origin of humankind had long been contested by alternative theories. As long ago as the first century BCE, the Roman poet Lucretius recorded the supposition of his predecessor, the philosopher Epicurus, "that our species, along with all the others, emerged as a result of random atomic mutations over a limitless expanse of time" and that humans "must have evolved only gradually and fitfully from savagery to civilization," as Stephen Greenblatt writes in *The Rise and Fall of Adam and Eve*. When the Spanish and Portuguese colonizers discovered the Indigenous population of Central and South America, this could have seriously challenged the Christians' biblical story, but the "savages" were dismissed as nonhuman, their speech regarded as animal noises. But again, there were cracks in the story. The Dominican Bartolomé de las Casas, for example, went so far as to suggest that the Americas were the site of the lost Garden of Eden and the humans morally superior, even faithful, even if not in the Christian sense, because they lacked the Catholic faith.

During the Renaissance period, it was dangerous for both Catholics and Protestants to put the Bible's chronology in question, but again there were exceptions. Ole Worm, who was surrounded by many great artifacts from Indigenous cultures, helped the Frenchman Isaac de La Peyrère in his research for his book first published in Latin as *Prae-Adamitae* and soon in English as *Men before Adam*, in which La Peyrère suggested that there was a creation of heathens and another separate creation of Adam as a progenitor of the Jews.

The decisive difference in the middle of the nineteenth century was the irrefutable scientific evidence that humans had evolved gradually. Although religious authorities initially resisted new insights from geologists, anthropologists, paleontologists, and archaeologists, these scientists left no doubt that humanity was far older than previously realized. It became clear that prehistory and early history—which were now divided into the Stone, Bronze, and Iron Ages—had been very long indeed. Was it also possible that its geographical origins had likewise been mistaken?

Meanwhile, Swedish zoologist Sven Nilsson would further attempt to classify humans and their history along "scientific" lines. In his 1862 book *The Primitive Inhabitants of Scandinavia*, the sociologically and economically oriented Nilsson laid out a model dividing human history into four stages of development: primitivism, nomadic animal husbandry, agriculture and settlement, and eventually high culture. A decade earlier, in 1853, the French diplomat and author Joseph Arthur de Gobineau had published the first half of his study *The Inequality of the Human Races*. He broke humanity down into the "white, yellow, and black" races—intending them to be understood in precisely that hierarchical order. Gobineau had a romanticized fascination for all things Oriental, and the following year brought an opportunity to further develop his ideas in a place that suited his fancy, when he was sent to Teheran as a secretary to the French diplomatic mission there. During his three-year stay, he threw himself into learning the Persian language and Persian history. Before he began working on his book, he had spent the preceding decade studying the leading philosophers of his time. In 1843, Alexis de Tocqueville, one of France's major liberal intellectuals and the author of *Democracy in America*, engaged Gobineau's services for a research project on the origins of customs and morals in modern Europe.

For Gobineau, humanity was in decline and racial intermingling was the reason. He loathed democracy and revolution and considered the Germanic peoples to be the creators of modern European culture, calling the Baltic coast and the Scandinavian Peninsula the "maternal lap of nations." He considered the "Aryans"—the "honorable men"—to be superior. Gobineau turned the term *Aryan*, which until that point had only been used in a linguistic sense, into an ideological cypher for "Indo-Germanic." The basis of this shift in meaning was a fateful conflation of the supposed congenital nature of a person ("race") and his or her culture ("language").

The idea of "Indo-Europeans" and of a family of languages linking Sanskrit and Persian with the European tongues originated in the late eighteenth century with William "Oriental" Jones, a British scholar of Indian languages and culture. The antithesis were the "Semites," with their Semitic languages, who were soon narrowed down to the Jews. It was von

Schlözer who coined the term *Semitic languages* for Arabic, Hebrew, and Aramaic, drawing on the name Sem, one of Noah's three sons. (Today these languages and others are categorized as *Afroasiatic.*) Widespread anti-Semitism in European society was an important force driving the reactionary Gobineau's popularity, notably in Germany, where Gobineau met several times with Richard Wagner. The author admired the composer, and the composer, in turn, was familiar with the author's work—the two were on the same wavelength. The fact that the Reichstag, the Parliament of Germany, granted equal status to Jews on April 22, 1871—a move opposed by jingoistic German nationalists—also played a role in public enthusiasm for Gobineau's work.

Gobineau's ideas took an even more bizarre turn in his later work *The History of Ottar Jarl* (1879). The book purports to follow the history of Gobineau's family back to Ottar, a ninth-century Viking. These beliefs about his ancestry explain why Gobineau claimed that the purest version of the "ur-race" lived on in his own lineage, the French Norman aristocracy, and among the Scandinavians. Gobineau's writings were first published in German in 1893 in translations by Karl Ludwig Schemann. It was of course no coincidence that this "skillful dealer in *Weltanschauung* [worldview]," as a recent researcher has dubbed him, was a racial theorist himself. Schemann founded a Gobineau society in Strasbourg in 1894, divesting the Frenchman's work of some of its pessimism and interpreting it through a lens of "Germanness." Schemann was a functionary in a variety of roles under the National Socialists and received the Goethe Medal for Art and Science from Hitler himself in 1937.

Gobineau, who later gained the inglorious title of "the father of European racism," was succeeded by others who developed his daring ideas further. For the social Darwinist Georges Vacher de Lapouge, Europe became what it was thanks to the presence of the "nordids," the people of the North. While Gobineau believed that they had originated in Siberia, Lapouge declared that the "cradle of the Aryans" was actually the "now-submerged Anglo-Scandinavian plain"—what is now the North Sea. The physician Ludwig Woltmann, who considered himself to be following in

Lapouge's footsteps, advanced the outlandish proposition that all important men of the past—including Dante, Napoleon, and Wagner—were Nordic. The prehistorian Gustaf Kossinna and the linguist Hermann Hirt took it as a given that the original home of the Indo-Germanic peoples was in northern Europe. Kossinna later became a member of the "Nordic Ring," founded in the mid-1920s by the racial theorist Friedrich Kurt "Hanno" Konopacki-Konopath.

As grotesquely ridiculous as such ideas may appear today, they were also hotly debated at the time. When it came to questions about the origin of the Aryans, the northern peoples, and humanity in general, clear distinctions between these groups were not always possible.

Americans, too, got on the bandwagon, reorienting their mental map of human origins away from the Semitic lands of the Bible and toward the "Aryan" North. The first president of Boston University, William F. Warren, studied in Berlin and taught systematic theology in Bremen before returning to New England to head up the Boston University School of Theology. Not satisfied with simply arguing for a northern origin story, in his 1885 book *Paradise Found: The Cradle of the Human Race at the North Pole*, he described a "primitive Eden at the North Pole." As "proof" of his bold assertions, Warren offered very liberally interpreted "evidence" he claimed to have discovered in ancient Egyptian, Babylonian, Indian, Persian, Roman, and even Japanese and Chinese texts. Ironically, he kicked off the foreword by declaring, "This is not the work of a dreamer."

The German physician and anthropologist Rudolf Virchow traveled to the Caucasus in 1881 to test just how credible the much-discussed theory of an Armenian Noah's ark really was. But the anthropometric measurements he collected left him "with a certain sense of disenchantment." According to his collected data, the people he met had no particular connection to those of Celtic, Slavic, or Germanic heritage. The physical differences were simply too great. A few years later, Virchow performed a comprehensive study of the skulls of schoolchildren. His findings showed that there were no physiological differences between Jews and Gentiles. Furthermore, he demonstrated that less than a third of Germans—whether Jewish or

Christian—had the blond hair and blue eyes requisite for the supposed "Germanic" type.

Did humanity really emerge from the North? In his 1906 book *The North Pole: Homeland of Peoples*, the writer Georg Biedenkapp drew on a study by the Indian politician Lokmanya Bâl Gangâdhar Tilak. In *The Arctic Home in the Vedas*, which had been published in Poona in 1893, Tilak expounds the theory that a lost Indo-Germanic civilization previously existed at the North Pole and that at the time the climate there was less severe. Biedenkapp was convinced that "the beginning of astronomy, the invention of the wheel and the wagon, and the onset of study of the natural world in the first place seems more plausible assuming the impressions and observations one would gain at the North Pole."

Preposterous ideas like Warren's and Biedenkapp's attest to the human longing observable in many societies past and present to spin a tale of glory and grandeur around one's own origins. Beyond that, they also represent an attempt to create a clear divide from the peoples of the South or East—depending on the particular situation—by those who had come to consider them "barbaric."

Today, the origins of humanity have conclusively been located in East Africa. Also, there is scientific evidence that vast sections of the Northern Hemisphere were covered in a thick sheet of ice 2.8 million years ago, ruling out the idea that *Homo sapiens* originated there. The proto-Indo-Europeans, a hypothetical prehistoric population in Eurasia during the late Neolithic period (approximately 4000 BCE), have been traced back to the Pontic-Caspian steppe between the northern shores of the Black Sea and central Asia. From there, these people's descendants migrated to Anatolia, the Aegean, northern Europe, and southern Siberia.

The Tactics of
Indigenous Peoples

The term *esquimaux* or *Eskimo*, the pejorative designation under which the Inuit were previously known, can be traced back to a less-than-flattering Canadian Native American word meaning "eater of raw meat." Accounts of human "curiosities" from the High North sporadically made their way to Europe long before Europeans began to take any serious interest in the region or to colonize it. In the late sixteenth century, King Christian IV of Denmark and Norway captured a number of Inuit people in order to examine them more closely. The English seafarer Martin Frobisher, who explored the Northwest Passage in 1576, also committed such acts of barbarism. In Greenland and parts of what is today northern Canada, fierce battles broke out with Inuit whom Frobisher suspected of kidnapping members of his expedition. He took several of these Indigenous people captive and brought them to England, where they were robbed of their dignity and displayed like trophies. One of the prisoners, a man named Kalicho, was forced, using whatever forms of coercion were necessary, to demonstrate his hunting and kayaking skills in Bristol. He shot two ducks on the Avon with a bow and arrow and was then made to eat their raw meat before an assembled audience. The journey south would end fatally for Frobisher's captives. They couldn't adapt to the English climate and had no natural immunity to local diseases. They all died. As American polar researcher Charles Francis Hall documented three hundred years later, the Inuit of Iqaluit, the capital of Baffin Island, still told of their battles with Frobisher's men—evidence of the robustness of oral history and the persistent legacy of historical trauma.

The European exploration and conquest of the North massively changed the lives of the Indigenous populace. It was only in the late nineteenth century that Westerners began to develop even a rudimentary understanding of Inuit culture.

Initially, the Inuit resisted European encroachments, but the closer we get to the present, the more they were induced, sometimes by force, sometimes with goods or money, to assist Europeans, Americans, and Russians, who often needed their help to survive in such hostile climes. Erasmus Augustine Kallihirua, who in 1850 accompanied Sir John Franklin's polar expedition as part of the "assistant crew" under Captain Erasmus Ommanney and was later given the name Erasmus York, became known around the world. The mission's main task was to investigate rumors that Indigenous people had massacred the survivors of an expedition that had gotten stranded in the Arctic ice. At the alleged scene of the crime, the Wolstenholme Fjord in upper northwest Greenland, the crew found no evidence of any such slaughter. Kallihirua then returned with the expedition to London, first going to St. Augustine's College of the Church of England in Canterbury, where he was trained as a missionary. He quickly learned to read and write and helped Captain John Washington revise his book *Eskimaux and English Vocabulary, for the Use of the Arctic Expeditions*. In 1855, Kallihirua traveled to St. John's, Canada, to continue his study at Queen's College. But he died before he could make a trip to Labrador, where he was supposed to work as a missionary among the Inuit inhabitants.

A four-volume study of the lives of the Inuit acquainted readers with their traditions, myths, and stories and disproved the predominant notion at the time that the Arctic was a region without history, even though there was no written documentation as there was in Europe. The *Kaladlit Oka-lluktualliait* (or *Greenland Legends*) was published in Godthaab, in southern Greenland, by the Danish geologist Hinrich Johannes Rink, whom the Danish royal family had sent to the island to record the oral narratives and research the traditions of the Inuit. He wrote his text in both West Greenlandic and Danish. The book was illustrated by Aron from Kangeq, a seal and walrus hunter who lived in that town's Unitas Fratrum mission. Aron, who suffered from the tuberculosis going around in Greenland at the time, was restricted to his bed, receiving papers, pens, and other drawing implements from Rink so that he could make his woodcuts. The four volumes of Rink's work are full of scenes of everyday life and reports of conflicts between the Inuit and Norse settlers between the tenth and fifteen centuries. The Europeans, however, eventually starved to death during the harsh winters or left Greenland, if they were able to, as the climate deteriorated in the late Middle Ages, making the voyage from Greenland to Norway increasingly difficult.

How did the paradigm shifts in the natural sciences affect how Indigenous people were seen? As of the mid-nineteenth century, when people began dividing history into the Stone, Bronze, and Iron Ages, the Inuit were assigned to the Stone Age. The idea that these people practiced a primitive stage of human communal life made them all the more attractive to an audience hungry for sensationalism. It was, of course, part of the larger colonial framework. In 1876, a group of Inuit were shipped from Greenland to Germany, where they were exhibited as an attraction in the Berlin Zoological Garden. Museums also "showed" these people. As late as 1896, polar researcher Robert E. Peary brought three men, two women, and a boy named Minik to the Museum of Natural History in New York. Some twenty thousand curiosity seekers turned out to welcome the ship and take a gander at these exotic foreigners upon their arrival. At the museum, they were questioned, examined, and measured. Tragically, within a few months, four of the Inuit died of lung infections. Their remains were kept in the museum archive until 1993. Years of research were required to

Kaladlit Okalluktualliait (Greenland legends, 1859–1863) was the first book printed in Greenland showing readers the life and the myths of the Indigenous population. *Courtesy of William Reese Company, New Haven, CT*

confirm that they came from the Qaanaaq region in northwestern Greenland, where the remains were finally returned for traditional burial.

The assistant curator of the museum who asked Peary to bring an Inuk from Greenland was the German-Jewish cultural anthropologist Franz Boas, who had traveled to Baffin Island in 1887 to research the Inuit pop-

ulace on the Cumberland Sound. Boas was a man of many contradictions. Best known for his groundbreaking ideas on cultural relativism, he
took a greater interest than anyone previously in the Inuit, viewed concepts
of race as socially constructed myths, and opposed the virulent racism of
his day—as early as 1894, he had taken a stand against scientific racism in
front of the American Association for the Advancement of Science—and
became known as "the father of American anthropology." At the same time,
he was deeply implicated in the activities of the museum and seems to have
been indifferent to the fate of the people so inhumanly and fatally put on
exhibition there. Rather incongruously, he staged a mock funeral for Qisuk,
the father of the boy, while at the same time having his body dissected and
kept in the museum. In 1909, when a journalist queried Boas about what
had happened, Boas saw "nothing particularly deserving severe criticism"
and defended the decision to keep Qisuk's remains: "Minik was just a little
boy, and he did not ask for the body. If he had, he might have got it." We now
know that Minik did ask for his father's remains to be returned to Greenland in 1906, but the museum denied being in possession of them.

Naturally, centuries of experience with hostile climatic conditions meant
that the Inuit were far superior to the European interlopers in the art of survival in the Far North. But the leaders of early Arctic expeditions were too
arrogant to learn from Indigenous people, even when their own lives were
on the line. Typical of this uncompromising attitude was a terse statement
by British explorer and president of the Royal Geographical Society Sir Cle-
ments Markham about travel in the Arctic in 1888: "No skis. No dogs."

Attitudes began to change around the turn of the century. One person who promoted a new view of the Inuit was Canadian adventurer Vil-
hjálmur Stefánsson, who hailed from the heavily Icelandic town of Gimli,
Manitoba. He made three early-twentieth-century Arctic expeditions and
blamed the members of Franklin's final disastrous "lost expedition" for having stuck too rigidly to their own familiar habits. They had hunted for sport
and not as a means to procure fresh meat, Stefánsson found, and the frozen
lemon juice they had brought with them lost its capacity for combating
scurvy after six months. The typical symptoms of apathy and exhaustion

had gone unrecognized, and the explorers had died of malnutrition in a region in which the populous Inuit had survived for generations.

Stefánsson's 1921 *The Friendly Arctic* was the result of a five-year Arctic expedition in which he took a knowing look at the patterns various generations of Arctic voyagers had followed. Stefánsson identified four stages, from complete ignorance about the special conditions of the region to complete acceptance of them. If Stefánsson is to be believed, staying alive in the Arctic was primarily a question of attitude. "When the polar regions are once understood to be friendly and fruitful, men will quickly and easily penetrate their deepest recesses," he wrote. Stefánsson was convinced that this was simple. All it required was to copy in detail the Inuit, who were the best example of how to survive the Arctic. Stefánsson never tired of stressing how crucial fur clothing, light sleds, and skill in handling dogs were for living and traveling in the icy Arctic landscape. The idea was not to wage a losing battle against the climatic conditions, but to adapt to the rhythm of Arctic life. When he fell ill during his expedition, probably of typhoid, he refused to follow the conventional wisdom of the day and instead consumed raw fish: "This seemed to do me good and next morning there was no fever." But the North had more to teach him, as he recognized in time: "My first year in the Arctic I saw everything through a haze of romance and did not for a while realize that it was a very commonplace country. But during the nine more years I spent there the realization kept gradually growing on me that one of the chief problems of the world, and particularly one of the chief problems of Canada and Siberia, is to begin to make use of all the vast quantities of grass that go to waste in the North every year. The obvious thing is to find some domestic animal that will eat the grass. Then, when the animal is big and fit, it should be butchered and shipped where the food is needed."

Stefánsson's portrait of the Arctic was full of light and confidence and contained some ideas that would raise a smile today, including the one just quoted from *The Northward Course of Empire* (1922), which seems a bit like a harbinger of the battle for raw materials going on in the region today. Stefánsson went beyond just considering the Arctic's "fitness to become the world's chief storehouse of domestic meats," prophesying that the Norwegian Sea would become something of an Arctic Mediterranean, the future center of an "innovative society." He may well not have realized that the development he predicted and promoted would change not only the character of the region but also the traditional Inuit way of life he so greatly admired. Stefánsson was a man of contradictions, but he played an undeniably major role in convincing politicians of the significance of the North, especially in Canada, a nation that is crucial to northern identity, even if the majority of its inhabitants live along its southern border with the United States.

The legendary documentary film *Nanook of the North* (1922) opens a window on the life of the Inuit people in the Canadian North. Robert J. Flaherty accompanies an Inuit by the name Nanook and his family in the Quebec Arctic for several weeks, recording their everyday life and the perils they face. Despite his sympathetic approach to his subjects, critics pointed out that Flaherty had arranged scenes to make them more dramatic, had falsified names and relations, and had depicted the Inuit as childlike, naive, and backward. In one scene, a fur trader plays a gramophone for Nanook, which Nanook studies. After hearing the sound, he takes the LP record and holds it to his ear, as though expecting sound to emanate from it. At the same time, scholars have documented that Nanook himself collaborated extensively with Flaherty in planning the scenes of the film. Still, it is argued that the film adopted a colonialist attitude that worked to legitimate Flaherty's and the audience's putative superiority.

Prior to the twentieth century, Western women generally kept their distance from the Arctic. A remarkable exception was Isobel Gunn, from the Orkney Islands, who, after meeting an employee of the Hudson Bay Company, joined the firm in June 1806—disguised as a man named John Fubbister. Gunn became the first recorded woman to set foot on Rupert's Land, a part of the British Empire named after Prince Rupert of the Rhine in what is now western Canada. Her true gender was first revealed shortly after Christmas in 1807, when to the bewilderment of all those around her, she gave birth. From that point on, she called herself Mary Fubbister. She was transferred to Fort Albany, in Ontario, where she worked as a wash-woman for a time, before eventually returning to Scotland.

As Angela Byrne points out in *Geographies of the Romantic North* (2013), travelers to the higher latitudes had observed Indigenous people who—according to the voyagers' understanding—could not be easily cate-gorized as belonging to either gender. British Arctic explorer John Franklin, for example, wrote in 1823 about a person who had "supernatural abili-ties," became a tribal chief, and went by the name of Manlike Woman. This echoes the two-spirit identity known from some First Nation societies, for-merly designated with the derogatory term "berdache." As Byrne writes, "the north was a place with supernatural associations, a space in which scientific travelers were alerted to the limitation of accepted geographical and climatic notions, and a cultural zone that permitted the construction of mediated and liminal physical and cultural identities."

Around the turn of the twentieth century, the Arctic began to attract increasing numbers of curious travelers, male and female. The Canadian educator and author Agnes Deans Cameron, who came from a family of Scottish immigrants, is thought to be the first White woman to reach the Arctic Ocean by land. She was accompanied by her niece and kept a type-writer and a camera with her. All told, in the spring and summer of 1908, taking the great waterways, she covered tens of thousands of miles and reached the delta of the Mackenzie River in the Northwest Territories. In *The New North: Being Some Account of a Woman's Journey through Canada to the Arctic* (1910), she wrote: "Canada has a third dimension, a diameter that cuts through the Belt of Wheat and Belt of Fur, beginning south at the international boundary and ending where in his winter-igloo the Arctic Eskimo lives and loves after his kind and works out his own destiny. This diameter we are to follow. To what end? Not, we hope, to come back like him who went from Dan to Beersheba to say 'All is barren,' but to come near to the people, our fellow-Britons, in this traverse section of a country big-ger than Europe. We want to see what they are doing, these Trail-Blazers of Commerce, who, a last vedette, are holding the silent places, awaiting that multitude whose coming footsteps it takes no prophet to hear."

Agnes Deans Cameron was also a passionate hunter. *Cameron,*

Agnes Deans. The New North: Being an Account of a Woman's Journey through

Canada to the Arctic. *New York: D. Appleton and Co., 1910.*

Cameron was particularly fascinated by the transitional zones between wilderness and industrial settlements, where whalers and Inuit slaughtered great numbers of whale and seal. One of her photos shows Inuit children playing the world's "northernmost game of football." Vividly written, *The New North* became a best seller. Pointing out that this part of the North had enormous economic potential that needed to be "discovered" in that sense and gifted with a vision of the future and some genuine understanding of the Inuit, Cameron energetically rejected the clichés of her day: " 'The Eskimo is a short, squat, dirty man who lives on blubber,' said text-books we had been weaned on, and this was the man we looked for. We didn't find him." A few pages later, she writes: "By natural gifts and temperament the Eskimo is probably the most admirable, certainly the most interesting, and by circumstances the most misunderstood and misrepresented of the all the native races of America."

Cameron was passionate about trying to make people aware that the High North needed protection, with the numbers of harbor seals and salmon dwindling and bowhead whales threatened with extinction. She encouraged her readers to plant trees to compensate for areas they deforested. Rather incongruously for an environmentalist so far ahead of her time, she posed for a photo in her book with the trophy of an elk.

A Distant Atlantic Island

Because of its geographical isolation, Iceland possessed a special status in the North. For a long time, it was considered the last charted land before the Northwest Passage, a wild place that was—to put it mildly—not exactly blessed with natural resources and that was home to barbarians. Still, the island nation, which was colonized by both Norwegians and English and Irish settlers, was known not just for its great trove of Old Norse writings but also for natural spectacles unlike those anywhere else in the North.

Early visitors to Iceland were struck by what seemed to be its backward culinary specialties. In 1699, during the time when Iceland was still a Danish colony, Dutch ship captain C. G. Zorgdrager traveled there and wrote a travelogue full of strange illustrations, among them a depiction of a joint of lamb on a rope being roasted. Older descriptions of Iceland were full of smells most visitors found unpleasant: dried fish, split sheep's heads

Iceland with somewhat exaggerated features from Eggert
Ólafsson and Bjarni Pálsson's travel report, 1772.

Courtesy of Wolfgang Horner

scorched when the wool was removed, sour mutton testicles, blood pud-
ding, smoked skate, putrified shark, and fermented foods.

Hamburg merchant Johann Anderson had nothing good at all to say
about the island. Although he never saw it with his own eyes, Anderson
had no problem publishing his voluminous 1747 book *News from Iceland,
Greenland and the Davis Strait*, which reads like a compilation of natural catastrophes and nightmarish visions. On alleged Icelandic customs,
he wrote: "Their favorite drink is consistently brandy, with which young

and old, man and woman, sully and intoxicate themselves most disgrace-
fully. As they go about their extremely arduous and difficult work on sea
and land, their consolation, motivation and main aim is to catch and clean
something that they can trade for brandy, their beloved brandy, the next
time Danish ships dock." Contemporary readers no doubt remained unsur-
prised at Anderson's assertion that Icelanders didn't feel the "slightest drive
to explore the arts and sciences." Anderson's account directly inspired
another one by Niels Horrebow, who spent two years in Iceland in the service of the Danish Crown and published his *History of Icelandic Geography*, first in Danish in 1752 and soon after in English, French, Dutch, and
German. In the late nineteenth century, Icelandic geographer and geologist
Torvaldur Thoroddsen wrote of Horrebow "credibly rejecting Anderson's
flights of foolishness and describing the country better and more precisely
than had been done in any book previously." For his book *The History of
Icelandic Geography*, Thoroddsen examined all the foreign accounts of his
homeland he could get his hands on.

Icelander Matthías Jochumsson (1835–1920), who often traveled around
Britain holding lectures, was cited as saying: "Well, Iceland has no army, no
apples . . . no atheists; no bridges, no banks, no beggars, no Baptists . . . no
corn, . . . no clubs, no cathedrals; no dukes, no diplomacy, no dynamite; no
electricity, no ambassadors, no elephants, no exchequer; no fabrics; no gas,
no gamblers, no gibbets, no gallows, no generals; no hospitals (except one),
no hydrophobia, no hogs, no heterodoxy; no inns, no infirmary . . . no loco-
motives . . . no laureate; no magazines, no manufactures, no museum, no
monks, no Magna Carta; no nihilists . . . no nobility, no night in May, June
and July." The final points on Jochumsson's list remain valid today; all of
the other ones would later have to be revised. So what did attract travelers
of the nineteenth century to this island located on the seam between the
American and Eurasian tectonic plates?

Ebenezer Henderson was the first British explorer known to have spent
a whole winter on Iceland in 1814–1815. He made his voyage there after
establishing a bible society in Copenhagen. This missionary, who was
familiar with the Scandinavian languages as well as Russian and several

Semitic and Asian ones, was chiefly interested in swiftly spreading the "holy oracle" among the island's populace. His two-volume book *Iceland: Or a Journal of a Residence in That Island* (1818) is a multifaceted travelogue concerned with everything from Icelandic history and education to geological topics like volcanism. "The general aspect of the country is the most rugged and dreary imaginable," wrote Henderson. "On every side appear marks of confusion and devastation, or the tremendous sources of these evils in the yawning craters of huge and menacing volcanoes. . . . These [huge mountains of perpetual ice], which naturally exclude the most distant idea of heat, contain in their bosom the fuel of conflagration, and are frequently seen to emit smoke and flames, and pour down upon the plains immense floods of boiling mud and water, or red-hot torrents of devouring lava." Henderson went on to list Iceland's "principle volcanoes," and at a later juncture in his book, he minutely discusses certain eruptions that were known at the time. The picture was one of omnipresent peril.

But Henderson's fear was tempered by his fascination with awesome natural spectacles. And his remarks about Icelanders' characteristic means of travel were surprisingly positive: "I was soon reconciled to the mode of travelling, on discovering that it was quite oriental, and almost fancied myself in the midst of an Arabian caravan. In fact, there exist so many coincidences between the natural appearances of this island, together with the manners and customs of its inhabitants, and what is to be met with in the East, that I must claim some indulgence from the reader, if I should occasionally allude to them, especially as they tend to throw light on many passages of Scripture." The tents he found in Iceland also reminded him of those of Bedouin Arabs. He displayed an impressive knowledge of Icelandic writing, above all *Landnámabók, The Book of Settlements*, which he characterized as going "with the greatest minuteness into the circumstances and transactions of the original settlers." According to him, in 860 CE, a storm drove a notorious Norwegian pirate named Naddodd to the Icelandic coast, and upon revisiting the island he had accidentally discovered, named it Snæland (Land of Snow). This was long before it was given the "repulsive name of Iceland." Henderson also glowingly describes the early formation of the Icelandic state: "So admirably did they distribute the different powers of government, that their mutual rights were secured without any compromise of personal liberty." Henderson was particularly captivated by the Icelandic ideal of freedom: "We here behold a number of free and independent settlers, many of whom had been accustomed to rule in their native country, establishing a government on principles of the most perfect liberty, and, with the most consummate skill, enacting laws which were admirably adapted to the peculiar circumstances of the nation."

In 1836, French author Xavier Marmier undertook a journey of his own to Iceland in conjunction with an exploratory mission of the Commission du Nord, for which he was recruited as a literature specialist. Marmier had taught himself some Danish and now wanted to research the Icelandic language and literature—more specifically, the connection between the land of the saga and its nineteenth-century reality. He made the passage from Cherbourg to Reykjavík on the corvette *La Recherche* in nine days. When he disembarked on May 30, he noticed the awful stench that pervaded the air. Marmier was shocked by the fish drying out in the open at the dirty harbor. But he was quickly won over by the hospitality of the Icelanders and soon had the opportunity to get acquainted with the *cabanes islandaises*, the simple dwellings made of peat and moss. He was astonished by the Icelanders' skill at getting by on the humblest of means. A "stove" was made solely of two large rocks. Whale bones and a horse skull served as chairs. And as elementary as this all was, the Icelanders were very educated. Almost everyone could read and write. Wherever he stayed, there were shelves with a Bible and a selection of books, reading material that Icelanders convivially passed around from neighbor to neighbor.

On his way to the Great Geysir, near Reykjavík, Marmier and his companions had to contend with fierce winds and midsummer temperatures below the freezing point. Anxious not to miss the eruption, they camped out near the geyser and took turns sleeping. After two days, they grew impatient and began throwing rocks and firing pistols at it—before long, such prompts had the desired effect. Then they pressed on to the Hekla volcano. The wind began to howl, rain poured down in sheets, and a thick fog surrounded the volcano, drastically reducing visibility. The travelers had needed to employ all their arts of persuasion to convince their guide that they should continue on. Then the gloom lifted, blue spots appeared in the sky, the sun came out, and as the expedition reached the volcano's peak, champagne they had brought along helped them forget their travails.

Back in Reykjavík, Marmier began studying Icelandic with the goal of reading the ancient writings in their original language: "It is a pleasant language to speak, and it's wonderful to see what degree of perfection it had attained in the eleventh and twelfth century. Today's Icelanders speak no other language than that of the Edda." Marmier was fascinated by languages, going so far as to assert that the basic vocabulary of English in all its hues mirrored that of Icelandic. His great dream was to compile an etymological dictionary of the Norse languages. But although Marmier repeatedly vowed to dedicate himself solely to his studies and forgo affairs of the heart, he couldn't help but to make repeated acquaintances with Icelandic women. In 1837, one of his lovers, a woman by the name of Málfríður, gave birth to a son she named Sveinn Xavier.

Four months after returning to France, Marmier completed his *Letters on Iceland*, which is still considered a seminal document of Icelandic social conditions at the time. Marmier wrote: "There exists between the poetry of a people and the land they inhabit, the nature surrounding them and the heavens under which they live, a close connection which very few books are able to depict and one has to have experienced in person in order to be able to feel it." The many editions of Marmier's book attest to the great influence it must have had. He even succeeded in making his mark on Icelandic literature—at a time when very few foreign visitors made their way to the island.

The popular Viennese travel writer Ida Pfeiffer also wrote about the explorations of the North in general and Iceland in particular in an 1845 book. After a storm-rocked eleven-day voyage, Pfeiffer arrived on the island from Copenhagen, hoping to find "Nature in a garb such as she wears nowhere else." Pfeiffer continued: "The shores of Iceland appeared to me quite different from what I had supposed them to be from the descriptions I had read. I had fancied them naked, without tree or shrub, dreary and desert; but now I saw green hills, shrubs, and even what appeared to be groups of stunted trees. . . . The supposed groups of trees proved in reality to be heaps of lava, some ten or twelve feet high, thickly covered with moss and grass" (from *A Visit to Iceland and the Scandinavian North*).

Pfeiffer set out on horseback to get a look at the picturesque fields of lava: "I could not tire of gazing and wondering at this terribly beautiful picture of destruction." At one point she offered the following characterization of her guide: "She is above seventy years of age, but looks scarcely fifty; her head is surrounded by tresses of rich fair hair. She is dressed like a man, undertakes, in the capacity of messenger, the longest and most fatiguing journeys, rows a boat as skilfully as the most practised fisherman, and fulfils all her missions quicker and more exactly than a man, for she does not keep up so good an understanding with the brandy-bottle. She marched on so sturdily before me, that I was obliged to incite my little horse to greater speed with my riding-whip."

Pfeiffer trained an acute, if critical, eye on the customs of the Icelanders she encountered. In her view, the people's dignity was by no means innate and quickly shaded over into stiffness: "In Hamburg I had already noticed the beginning of this dignified coldness; it increased as I journeyed farther north, and at length reached its climax in Iceland." After the end of one social encounter, she had trouble finding the door to leave, with the host declining to see her out—to say nothing of a servant being on hand to guide her: "To be well received here it is necessary either to be rich, or else to travel as a naturalist." An ironic undertone can be detected in this remark, because Pfeiffer is known to have had a passion for butterflies (of which there weren't any in Iceland).

Pfeiffer's blunt account wasn't to the taste of all readers. The Icelandic geographer Torvaldur Thoroddsen wrote (presumably as a compliment) of her "masculine character and masculine diligence" but balked at her "moody and sullen temper." Thoroddsen objected to her criticism of the Icelanders and complained about her far-fetched hypothesis that Iceland had emerged from the sea in the year 79 CE after the eruption of Vesuvius, disputing her scientific rigor—a quality she, in fairness, had never claimed for herself.

Following in the footsteps of Ida Pfeiffer several decades later was Elizabeth Jane Oswald, who wrote in her 1882 *By Fjell and Fjord* of the "restrained loveliness of the North, which, if less striking at first, is more lasting and less deceptive than the glow of the further south." Oswald was moved to draw a number of astonishing comparisons: "Alone in Iceland you are alone indeed and the homeless, undisturbed wilderness gives something of its awful calm to the spirit. It was like listening to noble music, yet perplexed and difficult to follow. If the Italian landscape is like Mozart; if in Switzerland the sublimity and sweetness correspond in art to Beethoven; then we may take Iceland as the type of nature of the music of the moderns—say Schumann at his oddest and wildest; smaller in some ways, and more subjective, needing more from the observer, and yet with a suggestive beauty of its own, with something of weird sublimity about it, and also quaint dissonances."

Meanwhile, Ethel Brilliana Tweedie took a different, less poetic direction in her profound 1889 report *A Girl's Ride in Iceland*, which was republished in numerous editions. She not only recorded her personal impressions on paper but also augmented them with her knowledge about Iceland's ancient political system, economy, literature, and geology. Iceland was a very unusual travel destination in the circles in which Tweedie moved. "Iceland, to Londoners, seems much the same in point of nearness as the moon!" she wrote. "And there really is some similarity in the volcanic surface of both." Even the initial preparations were difficult: "Inquiry at a London ticket office whether the officials could give us any particulars as to our route was totally unsuccessful, the astonished clerk remarking: 'I was once asked for a ticket to the North Pole, but I have never been asked for one to Iceland.'" In the end, Tweedie secured a berth on a Scottish steamship, the *Camoens*, for some reason named after the famous Portuguese poet Luís de Camões.

The title of Tweedie's book points to an issue she would confront extensively, the question of whether it was proper for women to ride astride a horse or, in Iceland's case, a pony. "It is nearly four years ago since, from a hotel window in Copenhagen, I saw, to my great surprise, for the first time a woman astride a bicycle! How strange it seemed!" Once in Iceland, she returned to the topic: "Riding man-fashion is less tiring than on a side-saddle, and I soon found it far more agreeable, especially when traversing rough ground. . . . For comfort and safety, I say, ride like a man." Ultimately, Tweedie concluded: "Fashion is ephemeral. Taste and public opinion, having no corporal identity, are nothing but the passing fancy of a given generation."

Tweedie also devoted considerable attention to Icelandic culinary preferences, including what used to be considered the absolute delicacy, swan eggs. Otherwise, she noted that fish in many varieties was always on the menu—"at each port we touched, the smell of fish, fresh or dried, assailed eyes and noses in every direction"—while pork was absolutely unknown. "In consequence of this strange fact, bacon would be as distasteful to an Icelander as to a Jew or a Moor. In 1873 one pig was introduced into the island. People came from far and near to look at such a wonder of creation, and even after the butcher's knife had put an end to his eventful career he continued to live in the minds of the people, who still tell stories of the half human shrieks of the strange and marvelous animal as he bled to death. Indeed, that pig has now become historical, and, though he has the honour of being considered a myth, his memory will linger for centuries in popular tradition. Immortal pig!" Tweedie was not aware that pigs, along with goats, had been introduced by early settlers but had been found to be too sensitive to the harsh climate. Icelanders gave up raising them in the twelfth century.

On the one hand, Tweedie described Iceland as "Ultima Thule" and extremely backward, writing that "a visit to the country is like returning to the Middle Ages." At the same time, she wasn't blind to Iceland's progressivism in other respects: "The Icelandic women enjoy great liberty. Liberty of action, liberty of thought, and from the earliest times have always evinced great independence." This was the point that most distinguished Iceland from another country with which Tweedie believed she could discern much common ground: Morocco. "The Icelanders are grave and serious and so are the Moors, who display strange gravity and solemnity for people dwelling in sunny climes." In both countries, she noted, there were "public story tellers" going from village to village: "Iceland eight hundred years ago was an intellectual light in a world of darkness, and was teaching Europe—more, 'tis true, in the way of literature—while the Moors were teaching us advanced sciences. . . . Icelanders are intensely superstitious, love ghost stories, and are great believers in the 'evil eye.'" Last but not least, Tweedie was struck by the country's natural beauty, proclaiming that "the rich warm colouring of the landscape resembled rather some southern clime."

Tweedie also searched in Iceland for examples of a bird that had already gone extinct in her day, the great auk. She started in a museum or, more precisely, what remained of one, since "all the best curiosities had been carried off to Denmark." But she had no luck: "Not even an egg has been found for over forty years, although diligent search has been made by several well-known naturalists." She was forced to make do with an imaginary picture of the auk, a not-too-flattering one, perhaps intended to compensate for her disappointment at never getting close to one: "The Great Auk was never a pretty bird; it was large in size, often weighing 11 lb. It had a duck's bill, and small eyes, with a large and unwieldy body, and web feet. Its wings were extremely small and ugly, from long want of use, so the bird's movements on land were slow, and it was quite incapable of flight . . . [but] on the water it swam fast and well."

Victorians and Vikings

Because of the Vikings' early mobility, settlements, and trade relations, England, Scotland, Iceland, and Norway have close historical connections, and over the course of the nineteenth century, the British focus would shift markedly northward. English diplomat and author Edward Bulwer-Lytton praised the Normans as the "Greeks of the Christian world," born to lead the world. The idea that there was a historical bond between Europe and India, which is substantiated by the Indo-European linguistic connection, was quite unpopular in England, where colonialists had a low opinion of a people they had subjugated. The British clung all the more fervently to the North's Judeo-Christian legacy.

With the excitment surrounding Ossian's epic poems having died down somewhat, and doubts about his authenticity growing, a number of authors turned their attention toward Old Norse writings, whose provenance was beyond question. The Victorians, in particular, began taking a keen interest in the Vikings. The Old Icelandic word was *víkingr*, but questions were raised as to whether they should be called *vikings, vikinger, wikingers, wikings, wicings, wickings,* or *norsemen*. No easy answer was forthcoming. And although there was no convincing evidence that the Vikings had ever worn horned helmets, they were often depicted doing so in the nineteenth century because it gave them a wild, animalistic aura. It's far more likely that they protected their heads with semicircular or conical leather caps with iron bands that were pointed at the top so as to deflect sword blows. In a mid-nineteenth-century illustration of the *Frithjof Saga*, a heroic tale concocted around the turn of the fourteenth century, Swedish painter August Malmström did suggest horns or wings on his warriors' helmets. Carl Emil Doepler, the costume designer for Wagner's *Ring of the Nibelungen*, outfitted his singers with horned helmets, having been most likely inspired by the Celts or Gauls, who were thought to have worn them. The horned helmets of bronze, which were found around this time in Denmark, dated back to 1000 BCE—or around two thousand years before the Viking age.

Stories about such a rough-hewn warrior people fired the imagination, and many British people sought to establish connections between the Vikings and their own heritage. For example, a wild notion circulated that Queen Victoria herself was related to Odin and that the royal Hanoverian line included Ragnar Lodbrok, that famous Viking chieftain who was said to have met a terrible end in a pit of snakes in Northumbria, one of the many small Anglo-Saxon kingdoms.

The British sang Old Norse songs and read Old Norse writings. Iceland, Norway, Denmark, and Sweden were perceived as a large single cultural unit vaguely connected to Viking history. The identification with the North went so far that some British people adopted additional names that had a whiff of higher latitudes to them. Writer George Barrow, for instance, signed his name as George Olaus Barrow. Trips to Iceland and Norway became pilgrimages to putative places of origin, with the most popular destinations being those familiar from the sagas. Tourists visited the fjord on whose coasts Frithjof had wooed Ingeborg, a well-known scene from the

In 1877, Norwegian painter Oscar Wergeland imagined the Norwegians on their voyage to Iceland in 872 CE. *Nasjonalmuseet for kunst, arkitektur og design, The Fine Art Collections*

Frithjof Saga. English lords journeyed to western Norway to catch salmon and convinced themselves that the local fishermen were long-lost cousins with a common Viking origin. British aristocrats also killed thousands of bears and many more eagles for sport, although this didn't dent their reputation, as hunting was common among Norwegians, too, if not for "sport." The Germans and French preferred the Alps as a location for such "leisure" activities.

The relationship between Great Britain and Iceland was like that of a couple who were perfect for one another but never succeeded in consummating their relationship. Iceland was purported to be a country where medieval literature and history played a greater role than practically anywhere else and people read sagas out loud while they whiled away long winter nights spinning wool. This cliché was considered true not just of intellectual circles, but also in the country and throughout all social classes. The actual tradition was called *kvöldvaka*, which means roughly "evening entertainment."

Back in 1518, Denmark's impecunious King Christian II secretly asked Henry VIII to loan him one hundred thousand florins, offering Iceland, which had been part of Denmark since 1380, as collateral. Christian repeated his request twice, but his entreaties were always rejected. Curiously, Denmark tried to negotiate a similar deal in the seventeenth century with merchants from Hamburg but without attracting any interest, presumably because Iceland was simply too far away from Germany. In 1785, a Scot by the name of John Cochrane once again broached the idea of taking over Iceland, whose population had been hit badly by natural catastrophes (volcanic eruptions and an earthquake), causing widespread starvation and a wave of emigration. Benjamin Franklin wrote that because of volcanic eruptions in Iceland in 1783, "there existed a constant fog over all Europe, and a great part of North America." Cochrane drew attention to the island's sulfur deposits and its potential stocks of codfish and suggested that the British establish a penal colony there. He was supported by Sir Joseph Banks, the president of the Royal Society, who had visited Iceland in 1772. This powerful advocate, however, didn't focus on possible economic benefits but rather on liberating Iceland from "Egyptian bondage" at the hands of Danes. In 1807, after Denmark had allied itself with Napoleon, and Great Britain had seized Danish colonies in the West Indies and India, Banks was once again asked to cast a vote on the issue. Although he still viewed the idea positively, pointing out that Britain wouldn't even need to invade militarily, the suggested annexation of Iceland was rejected. Then, in 1810, Great Britain declared itself a protector of Iceland. But as the Royal Navy was allowed freedom of movement in Icelandic waters, there was no reason for a conflict with Denmark, which had only been a temporary British enemy.

Icelandic historian Erik Magnusson, who emigrated in 1862 to Great Britain, remained a coveted speaker on the medieval connections between the two countries for decades, someone who flattered English audiences by assuring them that their compatriots had been among the "wealthiest most civilized" settlers of his native island. He also advanced theories that the Old English heroic epic *Beowulf* had been brought to northern Iceland by an early settler from Northumbria. In 1875, when the Askja volcano erupted, burying the eastern part of Iceland under its ash and poisoning the soil for years, the cultural mediator Magnusson immediately solicited British donations to help the people of Iceland. Many Icelanders emigrated around this time.

William Sabine Baring-Gould, the Victorian author of several Icelandic stories, expressed hope for that northern island nation in his writing. While acknowledging the problems of laziness, greed, poor hygiene, outmoded agricultural practices, and dependence on Denmark, Baring-Gould saw frost, strong winds, and the study of Old Norse writings as effective antidotes to the degeneracy of his own society. But there were other reasons for British people at the time to seek proximity to Iceland and Scandinavia. For instance, Lord Charles John Spencer Garvagh, the author of 1875's *The Pilgrim of Scandinavia*, viewed a united Scandinavia as an important potential ally and hedge against the threat posed by a now unified Germany.

On both sides of the Atlantic, people were beguiled by the false notion that Columbus had sailed from Bristol to Iceland to investigate a potential passage to America. Victorians asked themselves whether Columbus had been aware of the Vikings' voyages to Vinland, and the question remains a bone of contention even today. One of the many Englishmen who had fallen under the sway of the North was William Morris, the leader and personification of the arts and crafts movement. He was fascinated by what he called "The Great Story of the North." He approached the phenomenon very differently than Wagner, though, which among other things was due to his musical tastes running closer to Beethoven. He owed his breakthrough as an author to his book *The Earthly Paradise* (1868–1870), whose most famous part, entitled "The Lovers of Gudrun," is an adaptation of the thirteenth-century Icelandic *Laxdæla Saga*. Morris taught himself Icelandic and later translated the *Völsunga Saga*, along with classical works like the *Aeneid*, the *Odyssey*, and *Beowulf.* Morris, who once said his hatred for modern civilization was what drove him and who categorically rejected everything that was considered progress in his day, was devoted to people he saw as living in and with nature.

On trips to Iceland during the spring and summer of 1871 and 1873, Morris rode throughout the country on Icelandic ponies. He fell in love with the landscape and discovered a preindustrial idyll, where people worked the land with traditional tools and methods that had long fallen out of fashion in his homeland. Although the Icelanders were very poor, in his eyes they had made the ideals of freedom and classless society a reality. Icelandic communities cared for the sick and the weak, and the country had produced an impressive body of literature. Morris traveled together with his Icelandic colleague Erik Magnusson, with whose help he had translated Icelandic texts, but he also departed from well-trodden paths and stayed with locals. On August 11, 1871, he wrote in a letter from Stykkishólmur: "I have seen many marvels and some terrible pieces of country; I . . . am now half an hour's ride from Holyfell where Gudrun died. I was there yesterday and from its door you see a great seat of terrible inky mountains tossing about: there has been a most wonderful sunset this evening that turned them golden though; the firth we look on here is full of little islands that breed innumerable eider ducks, and a firth we crossed yesterday was full of swans."

Despite aspects of the rough surroundings offending Morris's hypersensitive aestheticism, he felt as though he had found his true home, as the figures and places he had read about came to life before his eyes. Moreover, his historical knowledge didn't blind him to the natural wonders on view. He also became even more conscious of the contrast between Iceland and the Victorian society he hated so much, familiar as it was. His enthusiasm for a way of life not based on the achievements of modern civilization made Morris an outsider in his day but also, in retrospect, a precursor of movements that even today advocate individual forms of economic activity and the principles they entail.

When he returned from his Icelandic voyages, Morris began working on

Sigurd the Volsung and the Fall of the Nibelungs, a four-part epic set in Iceland that he called the "most glorious of stories." Intended to acquaint and enchant an English readership with the lives and loves of the characters from the sagas, it was published in 1876, the same year the complete *Ring Cycle* was performed in Bayreuth. But Morris was anything but a fan of the composer. Three years before, he had made his opinion of Wagner abundantly clear in a letter, writing that it was "nothing short of desecration to bring such a tremendous and world-wide subject under the gaslights of an opera: the most rococo and degraded of all forms of art—the idea of a sandy haired German tenor tweedledeeing over the unspeakable woes of Sigurd which even the simplest words are not typical enough to express."

In the final decade of his life, Morris became a revolutionary socialist. He would carry the impressions Iceland made on him to his grave. Morris contributed to the popular misconception that Iceland was governed by a parliament when the body in question was in fact more like a convening of tribal leaders to resolve conflicts. The democratic village society Morris depicted in his novel *News from Nowhere* was reminiscent of Iceland, although the fictional setting was not quite as cold. In all of these works, Morris was able to serve up an inspired combination of appreciation for artisan life and a love of the North that was so in fashion in his day—and that was reflected, for instance, in the many works of stained glass depicting Leif Erikson's discovery of Vinland commissioned by wealthy New Englanders.

And what of the Vikings, those mythic explorers and conquerors? Recently, our understanding of this legendary warrior people has become far more nuanced, and many a myth—including the allegedly horned helmets—has been dispelled. Rudolf Simek, professor of ancient German and Nordic studies at the University of Bonn and a critic of the representation of Vikings in contemporary popular culture, points out that we have only the flimsiest evidence of how men and women of Viking times might have looked: "There is no indication whatsoever that they had tattoos or piercings, except horizontally scratched teeth painted in black, the meaning of which is unclear." As can be gleaned from pictorial representations and carvings, Viking men sported all kinds of haircuts, from pot cuts to half-long wavy hair. "They had goatees, moustaches and full beards, but little braids are nowhere to be seen! Also, the floor-length hair of Viking women is likely to be wishful thinking, but they certainly had long hair—the longer the nobler—and Irish ribbon knots which would have needed hair needles or nets to stabilize them," Simek says. "As Danish women researchers stress these days, the clothing at least of the elite was more colorful than we had previously imagined, with colored woven ribbons and fur trims."

Vikings have traditionally been depicted as hulking figures, but measurements of Viking remains show that the men had an average height of 5 feet 7 inches and the women 5 feet 2 inches. Nor is there any truth to the idea that the heathen Vikings waged a religious war against Christianity, even if it may have seemed that way to the Christian monks they brutally attacked. Vikings were "only" interested in plunder, while the monks spoke of a war of faith as a way of enlisting support from their coreligionists. In truth, some evidence suggests that Vikings were fascinated by the figure of Jesus Christ, about whom they had learned from their prisoners and from missionaries, and even viewed the "white savior" as a deity equal in stature to the Norse gods Thor and Odin.

The myth of Viking invincibility is less the result of their actual, technical military superiority than their habit of launching raids to get their hands on valuable loot. Viking ships landed before the targets of their attacks had time to sound the alarm and disappeared just as swiftly. Also, these raiders can be imagined more like the highway bandits of their time than typical representatives of the culture from which they came; they represented only a part of the population. Many of today's researchers believe that most people known as "Vikings" subsisted on agriculture, fishing, and trade and spent their lives in the places they were born, although they certainly were capable of raising arms to defend their homes and honor. That hardly conforms to the image of seafaring warriors.

Did female Vikings do battle as well? The excavated "Birka warrior" in

Sweden suggests they did. An ax, a sword, two horse cadavers, and a board game were found in this woman's grave, and when it was discovered in 1878, excavators assumed the occupant had to have been a man. It would be more than a century before Swedish researcher Charlotte Hedenstierna-Jonson and her team would prove the opposite using DNA analysis—also proving how unable many were to imagine a world in which men and women were free of fixed gender roles and how often scientists misinterpreted archaeological evidence. On the other hand, the bones of the female warrior show no signs of any sword blows or other effects of direct participation in fighting. It's possible that the woman was a battlefield commander. But critics have also speculated that she may have been interred in the wrong grave. Some researchers think that Viking household chores were divided between the sexes and that there were Viking "househusbands," since large cooking pots and skewers were also found in the graves of men. While the role of female Vikings—including "spear women," as the Valkyries referred to themselves—has attracted a lot of research interest among modern-day scholars, it remains to be proved conclusively whether there was a division of labor between the sexes or if women and men really enjoyed egalitarian roles.

Arctic Mania and the Discovery of America

It has always been the thirst for knowledge that drove interest in the High North, as the region was largely terra incognita until the twentieth century. One of the fundamental works for the scholarly study of the polar regions is the two-volume *An Account of the Arctic Regions: With a History and Description of the Northern Whale-Fishery* (1820) by the Englishman William Scoresby. It contains not only a history of the Greenland whaling industry but also a compilation of what was known about this part of the world at the time, from typical fauna to the various forms of ice crystals. Scoresby accumulated his knowledge from his numerous voyages in the waters between Greenland and the Svalbard archipelago as well as from other sources. In 1822, he continued his explorations during an expedition to the eastern coast of Greenland, the last he would make to the Arctic before beginning a course in theology at Cambridge. Though by no means an academic, Scoresby attracted considerable attention with his observation that the temperature of Arctic waters is higher at some depths than it is on the surface, inspiring others with superior technological abilities to investigate such phenomena.

The whaling industry was primarily responsible for any outside interest in Svalbard—that is, before geologists such as Switzerland's Louis Agassiz discovered it as a fascinating area for research. Agassiz's studies of glaciers in the 1830s elicited huge interest. German industrialist Barto von Löwenigh also reached the region in 1827 aboard a sloop rented from the Russians—he traveled from the North Cape with a stop on the Norwegian island of Bjørnøya. Löwenigh can be legitimately considered the first tourist to the archipelago, and he published a pamphlet entitled *Journey to Svalbard* in 1830. Although he was most interested during his six-week stay in the Sámi, their reindeer, and their hunt for walrus, he was impressed by spectacular natural phenomena such as the "near constant Northern Lights, which spread east from the west and take the place of day" as well as the low temperatures and the strong winds ("flatulences of nature," he called them), which didn't allow much snow to fall. Although Löwenigh's records were hardly scholarly or systematic, forty years later German cartographer August Petermann accorded Löwenigh's voyage a "place of honor among northern exhibitions," adding that "its results are some of the most interesting and valuable insights we have ever had into this region."

Attempts to explore the High North were greatly bolstered around 1830 by technological improvements to ships. Several countries played a role: Great Britain, the United States, Germany, and even the Austro-Hungarian Empire. The desire to find northwest and northeast passages initially drove innovation, but although the economic interests involved in discovering navigable straits persisted, many were beginning to doubt that they would ever be found. Had the attempt to locate passages become an irrational pursuit, even an obsession fueled by senseless national competitiveness? they likely asked themselves. The fate of British seafarer John Franklin, who set off in 1845 with more than a hundred men to find the northwest passage, never to be heard from again, demonstrated that even experienced explorers could come to a tragic end searching for the elusive passages. Popular interest began to shift to the North Pole.

The central figure in this shift in the United States was Elisha Kent Kane. He had taken part in the First Grinnell Expedition, led by Edwin de Haven in 1850, in which two ships set sail from New York to find Franklin after desperate pleas for help from his wife. In May 1853, Kane left New York for the North Pole. Along the way, he endured two winters locked in ice before he and his remaining crew abandoned ship, traveling some 1,200 miles in sleds and small boats before reaching the safety of Upernavik, in northwest Greenland, in August 1855. Although this expedition didn't result in any groundbreaking knowledge and didn't make it any farther north than the 80th parallel, it took on major symbolic significance. Kane's journey contextualized the Arctic North as an American frontier, much as the West had been previously and the moon would become in the twentieth century. Kane's 1856 book *Arctic Explorations* sold two hundred thousand copies.

An important impetus for attempts at the time to push farther and farther north was August Petermann's theory that a warm polar current made the North Pole passable in winter. In Petermann's view, the Bering Strait offered the best access to the region, and despite their implausibility, his ideas enjoyed great popularity and were only conclusively refuted a few decades later. Before that, people refused to give up their faith in a navigable North Pole passage, just as they clung to the hope of finding out for sure what had happened to Franklin. Petermann, who lived for some time in England and was also a popular lecturer, never traveled any farther north than Scotland himself.

Without exception, the various nineteenth-century polar expeditions, the last of which set sail in 1879, were resounding failures. It would take another three decades, until 1909, for American explorer Robert Edwin Peary to reach the North Pole. Nonetheless, the Arctic mania that had seized exploring countries lasted until after the start of the First World War. It was given a powerful boost with the declaration of the First International Polar Year in 1882–1883, which included one of the most ambitious international research projects of the nineteenth century. Eleven nations launched fourteen expeditions, twelve to the Arctic and two to Antarctica. Ten Arctic research stations were established, three of them by Great Britain, the United States, and Germany on Canadian soil. Germany also set up six ancillary observatories in Labrador. Together they expanded our knowledge of meteorology, geomagnetism, and the northern lights. But it would be another half century until the Second International Polar Year.

A major factor in the increased American public interest in the European North and its history was the considerable number of immigrants from Scandinavia, particularly to the Great Lakes region and farther west. Between 1836 and 1915, more than three-quarters of a million Norwegians arrived there. Many of them proudly pointed out that Leif Erikson had reached and settled American soil five centuries before Columbus. In 1837, Danish archaeologist Carl Christian Rafn had created a stir in North America with his book *Antiqvitates Americanæ*, which proclaimed Erikson and the Vikings to be the true discoverers of the continent. It was published a few years subsequently under coauthorship with North Ludlow Beamish as *The Discovery of America by the Northmen in the Tenth Century*. Some time later, this theme would be taken up by Rasmus B. Anderson, professor of Scandinavian Languages at the University of Wisconsin-Madison. Anderson viewed the Norsemen as the precursors of the Pilgrims, who, he claimed, came from the "Norse" parts of England. Anderson also imaginatively proclaimed that Leif Erikson's brother Thorwald had been murdered by American Indians while attempting to settle Cape Cod.

"Yes, the Norsemen were truly a great people! Their spirit found its way into the Magna Carta of England and into the Declaration of Independence in America. The spirit of the Vikings still survives in the bosoms of Englishmen, Americans and Norsemen, extending their commerce, taking bold positions on tyranny, and producing wonderful internal improvements in these countries," wrote Anderson in his 1874 book *America Not Discovered by Columbus*. He located Vinland in the Narragansett Bay region in what is now Rhode Island, citing as evidence, among other things, the stone tower above the city of Newport. Rafn had speculated that the tower dated back

to the Vikings. (Archaeological examinations have meanwhile proved conclusively that the tower was built in the early eighteenth century.)

With the installment of a bronze statue of Erikson in Boston in 1887,
this historical narrative was given an official seal of approval. The statue
was located near the spot, across the Charles River from Harvard University, of Erikson's alleged settlement. His statue, gazing out toward the west,
still stands there today.

But this was not the end of the story. In 1898, the so-called Kensington
runestone was discovered southwest of the town of Alexandria, in northwestern Minnesota, picturesquely surrounded by the roots of an aspen on
a plot of land just acquired by a Swedish immigrant. The discovery gave
rise to speculation that Vikings had left the stone behind in the fourteenth
century, some 140 years before Columbus landed in the Caribbean. Its
inscription told of a group of Native Americans being attacked and driven
off: "Eight Geats [North Germanic tribesmen from southern Sweden] and
twenty-two Norwegians on an exploration journey from Vinland to the
west. We had camped by two skerries one day's journey north from this
stone. We were [out] to fish one day. After we came home [we] found ten
men red of blood and dead. AVM save [us] from evil." On one of the margins of the stone was written: "[We] have ten men by the sea to look after
our ships, fourteen days' travel from this island. [In the] year 1362."

In 1909, John Ireland, the bishop of the St. Paul archdiocese, interpreted
the letters "AVM" on the Kensington runestone as "Ave Virgo Maria," or
"Hail (Virgin) Mary," the second most important prayer in Catholicism
after "Our Father." Ireland's interpretation was hardly neutral; it was clearly
intended to elevate the status of Catholics. Though French Catholics were
the first Europeans to explore the region back in the seventeenth century,
by the turn of the twentieth century they had become outnumbered by the
late-coming Protestants, above all Scandinavians and Germans.

By that time, geologists, archaeologists, Scandinavian linguists, and historians convincingly proved that the stone was a forgery: the inscription
contains a term, "opthagelse farth" (journey of discovery) that wasn't in

At first glance, the Kensington Runestone may look authentic, but it was soon revealed to be a fake. *Photo by Mauricio Valle/Wikimedia Commons*

use before the sixteenth century, and the object clearly lacked the typical signs of weathering that would have been expected. Nonetheless, the controversy around the stone did indeed have the effect likely intended by whoever put it there. At a time when the Scandinavian immigrant community in the United States was struggling for acceptance, this artifact supported the idea that Viking and Scandinavian settlements in America dated back centuries, conferring legitimacy. A Norwegian immigrant named Hjalmar R. Holland made it his life's mission to find evidence that the stone was genuine and ensure it received the public attention he believed it deserved. In 1924, Republican Idaho congressman Addison Smith expressed his particular pride in the many northern European immigrants in his constituency. Referring to the people "in the cities of the East," he said, "We have ample room, but no space for such parasites." He also called them "slackers."

As late as 1952, Father James Michael Reardon wrote about what he called the "earliest origin" of Catholics in Minnesota. Reardon was driven by the same motive as Ireland: "Nearly six centuries ago a group of Swedes and Norwegians made a journey west from Vinland and camped beside a lake on what is now Minnesota soil. The written record of that amazing voyage, unique in the annals of travel, tells the story of the heroic and tragic wanderings of this group of Catholic explorers from the distant fjords of Scandinavia who, in their hour of peril, invoked the aid of the Mother of God in the first prayer of which we have any extant account in the Western world" (from Reardon's book *The Catholic Church in the Diocese of St. Paul: From Earliest Origin to Centennial Achievement*).

Ten years later, in the summer of 1962, the town of Alexandria celebrated the alleged six-hundredth anniversary of the stone. This was the zenith of its fame, and the stone was put on display together with a large sculpture of a human figure at the New York World's Fair of 1964–1965. As religious historian David M. Krueger writes in *Myths of the Rune Stone* (2015): "The Viking statue towering over the exhibit boldly proclaimed the superiority of the Nordic male body and likely served to invoke in the fairgoers a sense of nostalgia for an imagined past that was whiter than the present. Although the facticity of the rune stone was open to debate, the narrative contained enduring truths that resonated with a popular version of American history and culture under threat."

Over the course of the next few decades, doubts about the stone's authenticity receded ever further into the background. When the topic was broached, the result was usually little more than a mention of the artifact's "controversial" origin. Even today some people refuse to relinquish the idea that the stone is genuine and contains deeper insights yet to be deciphered. The insistent belief in the legend is sometimes accompanied by the conspiracy theory, popular in certain circles, that the "true" history of North America has been purposefully kept concealed from the public. A short reminder: No one knows where the Kensington runestone really came from.

There was a similar phenomenon in Canada in 1936. The Royal Ontario

Museum acquired two halves of a broken sword, a battle ax, and a metal rod purportedly discovered several years previously southeast of the town of Beardmore. After examining photos, European experts confirmed that these were Old Norse artifacts. Twenty years later, the son of the man who found them swore under oath that his father had stumbled across the objects in the basement of a house in Port Arthur and buried them at the location where they were subsequently "discovered," thus confirming growing doubts as to the artifacts' authenticity. It appears as though these supposedly ancient objects were brought to North America around 1923.

In 1961, Norwegian archaeologist Anne Stine and her husband Helge Ingstad unearthed an Icelandic-Greenlandic settlement from approximately the year 1000 CE with the name L'Anse aux Meadows (the bay by the meadows), on the tip of the Great Northern Peninsula on the island of Newfoundland. Possibly founded by Erikson, it was concrete evidence of European settlement in North America before Columbus. L'Anse aux Meadows was a temporary settlement, apparently used for only two or three years, if we believe the sagas. Starvation, internal fighting, or conflict with Indigenous peoples are all possible reasons why it was abandoned.

Roy William Neill's 1928 *The Viking*, one of the last American silent films, reinforced Leif Erikson's symbolic claim as the first White man to land on the shores of the New World. The film was released at a time when most immigrants to the United States came from regions other than northern Europe. Other films that adopted the notion that Erikson and not Columbus had "discovered" America included Richard Fleischer's 1958 *The Vikings* and Terry Jones's 1989 *Erik the Viking*.

Dramatic Cliffs and
Kaleidoscopic Waves

Prior to the nineteenth century, there were not many northern landscape paintings. Just as for mountains and seascapes, the taste for such scenes had not yet been formed. One of the rare exceptions is the work of Dutchman Allaert van Everdingen, from Haarlem, near Amsterdam, who came to Sweden in 1640 and then devoted himself upon returning home to depicting Scandinavia's sparse mountain landscapes and waterfalls in the style of Flemish landscape painting. But few of Everdingen's colleagues appreciated his subject matter. Around 1790, Swiss-English artist Henry Fuseli (also known as Johann Heinrich Füssli) painted his iconic *Thor Battering the Midgard Serpent.* Although taking up a popular myth of Norse mythology, it was most likely intended to express his support of the French Revolution—the serpent symbolizing the Kingdom of France. The North would first attract widespread artistic interest in the nineteenth century, when Norse tales and sagas increasingly exploded in popularity and were depicted throughout Europe in popular magazines, prints, and postcards.

As far as paintings of northern landscapes are concerned, Caspar David Friedrich is an important example for the first half of the nineteenth century. Born in the city of Greifswald, on the southern coast of the Baltic Sea, which at the time was part of Swedish Pomerania, Friedrich studied painting in Copenhagen. Contemporaries described him alternately as a "northman of few words," as a "melancholic Hyperborean [giant]," and as a person of "northern superiority and greatness," who commendably had "not a drop of French blood in him" and had never considered learning "one of the foreign modern languages." Friedrich's interest in the North as a source of inspiration was all-consuming, and with few exceptions, he gave the Italian motifs typical of his day a wide berth. He even named his son Gustav Adolf, presumably after Sweden's King Gustav Adolphus.

Friedrich may have never made it to the Arctic, but that didn't prevent him from taking it up as a subject. His paintings were full of darkness, shadows, and fog, phenomena prominently associated with the North at the time. By contrast, the South was flooded with light. An 1806 observer characterized his work as having a "northern preponderance." Despite rumors to the contrary, he consistently refused invitations to travel south. In any case, his 1816 reply to the invitation issued by his friend and colleague, the German-Danish painter Johann Ludwig Lund, was rather cryptic: "I could well imagine traveling to Rome and staying there. But I shudder to think about returning from there back north. In my mind that would be tantamount to burying myself alive. I have no problem with remaining in one place, without complaint, if that's what fate desires. But going backward contradicts my nature. My entire being rebels against it. . . . Fare you well under the milder skies and among the more sublime natural conditions."

Perhaps Friedrich's final remarks were ironic, or perhaps he wanted to avoid offending his friend with a brusque refusal? The often-praised quality of the light in southern Europe must have appealed to him and would have certainly influenced his work. Maybe he sensed this and didn't want to risk such an experiment. In another context, Friedrich scoffed: "Our German sun, moon and stars, our cliffs, trees and herbs, our plains, lakes and rivers, are no longer good enough for our genteel artistic judges. Everything has to be Italian for it to claim greatness and beauty." Vienna was as far south as Friedrich ever traveled in his life.

The island of Rügen on the Baltic coast, with its picturesque chalk cliffs that practically begged for Romantic depiction, occupied a special place in German culture as a sublime, melancholy, and fabled northern outpost. Although part of the Continental European landmass, geologically it was, together with the island of Møn, in the Danish section of the Baltic Sea, and the region around Dover, England, part of what had been a massive chalk plateau, of which, after a tectonic shift, only broken pieces remained.

In Friedrich's wake, others were infected with their love for northern landscapes. When Romantic painter Carl Gustav Carus, whose circle included Goethe and Alexander von Humboldt and whose favorite motifs were reminiscent of his friend Friedrich's, visited Rügen in 1819, he was struck by the "rich, powerful primeval nature of the North." He wrote: "One must abandon oneself, silent and true, to the monotonous landscape, look on in solitude as the waves roll into the echoing bays, follow the flights of the gulls, cranes and swans, listen to the rush and thunder of the surf, wander the thick beech forests among the monuments of Old Norse prehistory and gaze from the mighty chalk cliffs at the ships sailing in the distance across the kaleidoscopic colors of the ocean tides."

With Norwegian cruises becoming increasingly popular among Europeans and some affluent Americans, artists began sailing along and producing paintings for wealthy travelers. One such artist was the marvelously named Themistokles von Eckenbrecher, who was also fond of "Oriental" motifs. He made his first trip to Norway in 1882 and started painting majestic, darkly overcast fjord landscapes, very much in keeping with the taste of the Wilhelmine public. And among the most famous modernists to take on the North as a subject was French Impressionist Claude Monet, who traveled to Norway in 1895 to paint snow-covered landscapes.

And others ventured farther north. In 1869–1870, the officer and Alpine enthusiast Julius von Payer took part in the second German north polar expedition to Greenland. Shortly after, von Payer was one of the leaders of the Austro-Hungarian North Pole expedition of 1872–1874, financed by Viennese aristocrats, which discovered and claimed "Franz-Joseph Land," a group of islands east of Svalbard the explorers touted as "the northernmost land on earth." But the crew and passengers aboard the *Tegetthoff* (named after the Austrian admiral Wilhelm von Tegetthoff) paid for these triumphs by enduring two hard winters on board after the ship became stuck in ice and then drifted north. In the end, they had to start back home on foot and were eventually rescued by Russian seal hunters. Payer was euphorically welcomed back to his home city of Vienna, but jealous rivals soon began talking behind his back, questioning whether the islands he had discovered truly existed. Disappointed, he turned to art, studying in Frankfurt and Munich, where he created a cycle of paintings depicting Franklin's lost expedition. He later moved to Paris, where he continued to produce large-scale, often dramatically staged Arctic landscapes, before ultimately ending up back in Vienna. But he was never able to realize his primary dream of reaching the North Pole in a submarine.

"For God's Sake, Don't Look Down!"

I t took quite some time for Scandinavia to become a travel destination in the minds of ordinary western and central Europeans. Among the pioneers of this trend was the philosopher Henrik Steffens, the Norwegian-born son of Danish-German parents, who called himself "the Norwegian." Early in the nineteenth century, he went to the University of Halle and later inherited eminent philosopher Georg Friedrich Wilhelm Hegel's academic chair in Berlin—his students included no lesser figures than Karl Marx and Søren Kierkegaard. In his ten-volume memoir entitled *What I Experienced* (1840–1844), he wrote: "People form a more or less fantastic image of the lands of the rough-hewn North. My fatherland was rarely visited in those days. For travelers, it was located off to one side, as though beyond Europe. A trip to Norway considered almost the same as one to the coasts of Africa or Asia."

It was in 1818 that Mary Shelley published her iconic horror story *Frankenstein* (1818), framing the novel with the Arctic as an embodiment of the sublime and setting the end of the novel at the North Pole. Without retelling the entire story here, the monster murders Victor Frankenstein's fiancée on their wedding night and then flees. Victor pursues him to the Far North, where they play cat and mouse across the ice floes. Victor dies, and the creature survives, only to commit suicide by voluntarily floating away on the ice, leaving himself exposed to the deadly elements: "We perceived a low carriage, fixed on a sledge and drawn by dogs, pass on towards the north, at the distance of half a mile; a being which had the shape of a man, but apparently of gigantic stature, sat in the sledge and guided the dogs. We watched the rapid progress of the traveller with our telescopes until he was lost among the distant inequalities of the ice." Shelley's marvelously moody depictions apparently captured the imagination of her readers; in the years following the novel's publication, Arctic exploration for tourists began to take off.

The 1836 *Ladies Conversations Lexicon*, published by Carl Herloßsohn in conjunction with scholars and female writers, described this "strange and wonderful land" as follows: "Norway extends above Sweden's northwestern border like a bonnet of granite and porphyry atop the head of Virgin Europe. Previously it was a stone helmet, for the grey days of prehistory knew the tall, light-blond Normans as mighty ocean heroes across the seas and bold conquerors of places from distant Sicily to today's England. . . . Here is a land of contrasts: sublime greatness and idyllic charm, terrible wilderness and lively landscapes, short, scorching summer heat and long winter cold—all of these antipodes in direct contact with one another. . . . Harmlessly curious natives welcome foreigners everywhere with the well-meaning question: Who is this fellow—what does he want!" There is no record of how many of the lexicon's lady readership were sufficiently inspired by such flowery description to in fact take a journey to the High North.

Another early mediator between the Continent and Scandinavia was Anna Amalie von Helvig, the niece of Charlotte von Stein, the prominent friend and supporter of Goethe and Schiller in Weimar, Germany's most important intellectual center at the time. In 1803, she followed her husband, a Swedish colonel, to Stockholm, where she lived for several years and established a literary salon. In an 1819 letter, she wrote to Swedish author Esaias Tegnér with a flowery wish for the future: "May the day soon come when Germanic art and literature melts into one, and the Swedish language here, like the German one across the Baltic Sea, appear to be but familiar dialects of a common tongue. It is from the North that there seems to bubble up the fresh, lively wellspring destined to joyously nourish unclear, full-bodied waves, the partly sealed-off, partly labyrinthine source of our German literature, after we perhaps flatter ourselves that the electric sparks of related genius have awakened this new radiance of imagination from the mineshaft of its slumbering depths." Formulating her thoughts even more energetically, she wrote to Tegnér in 1821 of her hope "that the fresh North Wind will cure us of the humid Scirocco and Simoom of the South."

The decline in Scandinavia's political influence starting in the eighteenth century, its sparse population density, and its relatively low level of industrialization made it a magnet for people's longings for untouched nature and traditional ways of life. Painters depicted bucolic idylls, birch forests and mountain and ice landscapes, and contemporary composers followed suit. The musical equivalent to Romantic paintings were the works of the Norwegian Edvard Grieg and later, on the threshold between late romanticism and early modernism, Finland's Jean Sibelius. Tourists dreamed of discovering a place that seemed to them a book of fairy tales. Visitors found farming communities where happy people paraded in colorful costumes like Norwegian Hardanger bunads, traditional clothes. Whether it was in Norwegian Jotunheimen ("Home of the Giants") or the bucolic landscape of Dalarna in the Swedish heartland, curious travelers from big cities and foreign countries could lose themselves in a picturesque world reminiscent of an outdoor museum.

Both the German Ernst Moritz Arndt and the Dane Hans Christian Andersen journeyed to the Falun copper mines in central Sweden. Andersen compared the stench of sulfur in Falun with the smell he had encountered at the Solfatara Crater near Naples. Otto von Bismarck, the later mastermind of the German unification in 1871, hunted deer in Denmark and Sweden in August 1857. From the town of Tomsjönäs, he wrote back home to his wife Johanna: "Imagine the most barren region near Viartlum [then part of Prussian Pomerania]. Around one hundred square miles from one another, alternating regions of grass and moor and forests of birch, juniper, pine, beech, oak and black alders, sometimes impenetrably thick, sometimes sparse and thin. The whole landscape strewn with countless stones ranging in size up to blocks of cliff rock thick as houses, smelling of rosemary and resin. In between strangely formed lakes, surrounded by hills of heath and forest. Then you have Småland, where I find myself right now. The land of my dreams actually, unreachable to dispatches, colleagues and Reitzenstein nobility, but unfortunately also to you. . . . Still, I'll probably emigrate here someday."

Folkloristic landscape museums like the *Nordiska Museet* (Nordic Museum) and Skansen Museum in Stockholm, the *Norsk Folkemuseum* (Norwegian Museum of Cultural History) in Kristiania (Oslo), and the *Kansallismuseo*, the Finnish national museum in Helsinki, idealized and mythologized farming culture and became popular attractions in their own right. The employees of these "human zoos"—for lack of a more benevolent phrase for historical exhibitions about ordinary people's lives—went about performing "typical" activities. There were precedents for this in the national expos at the World Fairs. Unlike other European countries, who highlighted elite culture in their self-presentations, at the London Fair in 1851, Norway and Sweden presented puppets in folk costumes. In 1867, in the Parisian Champ de Mars, a green public space adjacent to the site where the Eiffel Tower would later be built, Sweden rolled out a Laplandic family hut replete with stuffed reindeer and wood carvings. All of this encouraged the view of these countries as primeval idylls, frozen in time.

Descriptions in popular histories and travel handbooks bolstered tourism. The first Baedeker travel guides for Sweden and Norway appeared in both English and German in 1879. Starting just before the middle of the nineteenth century, steamships regularly sailed routes between Kiel

Scandinavia was often seen as a living ethnographic museum.
This photo was taken by S. J. Beckett in Norway in the early
twentieth century. *Photo by S.J. Beckett, courtesy of Vestland fylkeskommune*

(northern Germany), Copenhagen, and Kristiania (now Oslo) on the one
hand and Hull (England) and Bergen on the other. Railroad construction
began in 1850, improving access to remote regions. Around 1875, travel in
Europe had become considerably more comfortable, and passports were
no longer required in most countries. Nonetheless, travelers had to accept
considerable compromises in accommodation. As late as the turn of the
twentieth century, foreign tourists still complained about the short, narrow beds, the heavy, sausage-shaped coverings, the lack of closets, nails
serving as coat hooks, and dirty chamber pots. In 1855, Karl Baedeker
wrote of Norway that "one travels here today in roughly the same fashion
as in Switzerland 50 to 60 years ago."

As early as 1860, the German zoological writer Alfred Edmund Brehm advised the readers of the popular magazine *Die Gartenlaube* (The Garden Gazebo): "Those who don't want to travel in old, overeducated Europe must go to Norway. Those of us from the interior countries no longer travel. We simply run after things. In the north of Europe, Norway in particular, people still travel. There, you answer only to yourself. There you feel self-sufficient. You leave behind all your previous circumstances and are liberated as soon as you set foot on that green peninsula."

Brehm was a man of his times. Despite his call for deceleration, the main thing was to cover the distance to northern Europe as comfortably and as quickly as possible. Toward the end of the nineteenth century, the Hamburg ocean carrier HAPAG began offering northern cruises to go along with those in the Mediterranean. Being anything but cheap, they allowed the company to compensate for shortfalls caused by the dwindling numbers of European emigrants to the United States. Some of these cruises took passengers beyond Norway up to the border of the Arctic Circle and to North America via Iceland. The locations people thought about when they cast a longing eye toward the North were oriented farther and farther toward extreme climatic regions.

And there was another development that drew aristocrats and many others to the higher latitudes. Starting in 1889, Kaiser Wilhelm II (his reign lasted from 1888 to 1918) headed off for several weeks every summer in his yacht, the *Hohenzollern*, for the Norwegian fjords—a habit he continued with few exceptions until 1914. Couriers and messengers with dispatches, connected to the highly developed Norwegian telegraph network, allowed him to continue to perform his duties of state. The magazine *Volk* (People) wrote of the monarch's 1889 trip: "The first man of all Germanic tribes greets those wonderful coasts on which Northland's warriors learned to subdue the seas and forge the courage to perform deeds of world historical importance. The skalds [Norwegian and Icelandic poets] will awaken in their graves. Hail to Jehoshaphat! There is no one like him anywhere on big blue sea. His men, they fight so far away." (Jehoshaphat was the son of Asa, the third king of the kingdom of Judah.)

Wilhelm's stated intention for his voyages was to maintain relations to

Germany's "neighboring and blood-relative nations." When he visited Kristiania (now Oslo) in 1890, he presented the Norwegian people with a larger-than-life statue of a Viking and was cited as saying: "Magic threads draw me to this broad-shouldered people, whose sagas and divinities expressed the most beautiful virtues of the Germanic people, manly loyalty and faith in one's king." Wilhelm added that he considered himself a descendant of the Vikings and felt as though he was "returning to his original native land." Every year, he invited around a dozen men to accompany him on his trip, describing his companions with his unusual sense of humor as his "bathing guests." A contemporary observer described the atmosphere within this select company as "the air of court with a nautical whiff."

The initially restless excursions of the young "travelling Kaiser," which took him from Kristiania to the North Cape, were peculiar events, combining his maritime and his Nordic proclivities. "Kaiser Wilhelm II's 'northland' cannot be found on any map," wrote the contemporary Scandinavian studies scholar Stefan Gammelien, hitting the nail on the head. "It is an imaginary, utopian region of the world, a pre-capitalist idyll inspired by Romantic adaptations of Old Norse sagas and their adaptation in the incipient travel literature in the early 1880s, which made Norway the center of the Northland." Molde, located between Trondheim and Bergen, profited most from the visits of the kaiser and his entourage. The city was known for its Swiss-style Grand Hotel and traditional Alexandra Hotel. People joked at the time that the only way to get a glimpse of the German emperor was to travel to Norway.

The kaiser's enthusiasm hardly came out of the blue. His political confidante, Philipp zu Eulenburg, who saw himself in the tradition of the court poets of medieval Scandinavia and himself wrote skald songs for voice and piano, introduced Wilhelm to the world of the North as a boy. The emperor was said to have learned large parts of Tegnér's *Frithjof's Saga* by heart.

What were Norway's major tourist attractions? Dating back to the days when Bergen was the country's most important city, there was the Håkonshallen, an imposing stone edifice built in the mid-thirteenth century by King Håkon Håkonsson. Over the centuries, the largest of Norway's medieval buildings repeatedly hosted events of national significance. But aside

The Norwegian fjords, with their dramatic contrast of mountains and sea stretching deeply inland, was a beloved destination for affluent Europeans beginning in the late 1800s. Painting of the steamship "Auguste Victoria" in Naeröfjord by Karl Paul Themistokles von Eckenbrecher.

bpk | Staatliche Schlösser, Gärten undKunstsammlungen Mecklenburg-Vorpommern | ElkeWalford

from the impressive wooden stave churches, the country didn't have many symbolically important buildings. Its main attractions were the fjords, first and foremost Geirangerfjord, which was deep enough to be navigable by large ships and gave travelers a spectacular view of the surrounding mountains, whose peaks could also be accessed by land. Norway was also known for its many waterfalls and picturesque natural sights like the Trolltunga (Troll's Tongue), a horizontal rock projection, also accessible by foot, 3,609 feet above sea level on the Sørfjord, and the Preikestolen (Pulpit), an eye-catching platform in the middle of a cliff with a lovely view of the Lysefjord. Above the Lysefjord, on the Kjerag plateau, there was also the Kjeragbolten (Kjerag Boulder), a 177-cubic-foot monolith wedged into

The Preikestolen (Pulpit Rock), high above the Lysefjorden, is one of Norway's major tourist attractions. *Photo by Odd Inge Worsoe, courtesy of Stavanger Turisforening*

a crack in the cliffs—a spectacular attraction that continues to draw tourists today. Tromsø, located within the Arctic Circle and mostly within the auroral oval surrounding the magnetic North Pole, where the sun doesn't rise for two months in winter, was known as an excellent location for viewing the northern lights. The same was true of Abisko, in the Swedish part of Lapland—the area stretching from northern Norway to the Kola Peninsula (Russia) and populated by the Indigenous, seminomadic Sámi.

At the end of the nineteenth century, the 1,000-foot-tall black cliffs of Cape North joined the ranks of these attractions. Its popularity began after a visit by King Oscar II of Sweden in 1873, which was followed by visits from Wilhelm II and Archduke Karl Ludwig of Austria-Hungary. As of 1893, it was possible to reach it via steamboat, and large cruise ships began including it on their itineraries. Traveling to this remote location by land remained a challenge. Because the cape is located on Magerøya Island, it is technically not the northernmost point of the European mainland. That honor goes to the Kinnarodden Peak a few miles to the northwest.

The vast expanse of the ocean, the special light and the spectacular rock—and, most probably, the promise encapsulated in its name—made the North Cape a popular destination. Trips there were often organized so that travelers arrived in the evening or at night and could enjoy the atmosphere at this European outpost. Anyone who has ever witnessed the midnight sun knows how it can bewilder the senses—much like when the window shades are lifted after a long flight and the airplane is flooded with light, although passengers still feel as though it's nighttime.

Journalist Robert Davidsohn scaled the cliffs in the region with a twenty-six-person team in the summer of 1884, warning its members, "For God's sake, don't look down!" Ropes were used for particularly steep stages "so that women, too, could make the climb." The Swiss physician Elias Haffter, who was on board the first voyage of the steamship *Auguste Viktoria* to Svalbard in 1899, recorded some of the minor dramas that took place at the time at the "northern edge of Europe." His visit began with a challenging climb. Once Haffter's group arrived at the base of the cliff, its members had to make their way up a steep, zigzagging path. Although the 360 passengers were lured by the prospect of a glass of champagne against the backdrop of the midnight sun, during a night without darkness, fewer than 100 of them braved the arduous climb. "We were particularly amused by a giant of a man, who strode out ahead of us like a conqueror certain he would be able to climb Europe's border stone as though it were child's play," wrote Haffter. "How soon we caught up with him!"

This was the reality of the sublime experiences tourists traveled to the North to find. After all the passengers had returned to Haffter's ship more or less in one piece, "the trip proceeded in the nighttime sun, as bright as day" to the Arctic Ocean.

At least during the nineteenth century, Finland was not usually part of trips to Scandinavia, perhaps because the landscape is not that dramatic compared with Norway and Sweden. The first travel guides exclusively devoted to this land of forests and lakes were published in the 1890s. Among the few earlier travelers was the adventurer Edward Rae, who in 1873, along with a companion, boarded a steamer bound for Trondheim, Norway, in Hull, then traveled on to the Lofoten Islands and from there crossed Sweden by horse and went to the northern part of the Gulf of Bothnia and Oulu, Finland. Along the way, he relied on Johannes Scheffer's book about Lapland from a full two centuries before. The most important differentiating factor of the country for him was the native language. Rae commented: "The Finnish tongue I think is the finest I have ever listened to. I have never been so struck with a language: to hear these illiterate boatsmen talk to one another in sounds that rivalled the most beautiful in the ancient Greek, made us jealous, and very ambitious to speak it with them. No weak mincing words, nor coarse gutterals: more dignified than the delicate French: more manly and strong than the soft Spanish. Their towns, rivers, hills, and villages have good names: Kardis, Haparanda, Muônioniska, Matarengi, Aâwasaksa, Torneå, Saimen, Wuoxin, Imâtra, are common instances: and I prefer them to Piteå, Luleå, Trondhjem, Molde or Levanger-Swedish and Norwegian names" (from *The Land of the North Wind—Or, Travels among the Laplanders and Samoyedes*, 1875).

It is impossible to say how far Rae and his companion got with their rudimentary Finnish. After all, the tongue is one of the Uralic languages, kin to Hungarian, and is not at all related to the Anglo-Saxon or Germanic ones. Still, his positive take on Finnish was very unusual for his time.

Rae's description of the "Finnish vapour-bath" is among the more detailed early records of what came to be known as sauna. He even had an attendant, "a decent hard-featured woman" who came into the wooden bathhouse "without the slightest embarassment or false delicacy, and bathed me much as if I had been in a Turkish bath." Rae added: "By-and-by she told me to mount by a wooden ladder to a small raised platform, when she threw a pailful of cold water upon the heated stones, and the hot steam came round me in clouds. I was directed to switch my limbs and shoulders with a bunch of birch-twigs, until the gentle perspiration came upon my forehead and face. Then I sat with my feet in a bucket of delicious cool water, while the bathing mistress poured soft water over my head and shoulders: then I was soaped and drenched again until I felt as clean as an ivory statue."

The Farthest North

I t was not just the cultured and sublime mythical North, refracted through romanticism, that stirred people's emotions around the turn of the century. People were also attracted to the concept of an unsullied, white, unpopulated, symbolically charged region—"the virgin snow and the untrodden land," in the words of Danish cartographer Godfred Hansen, who had accompanied explorer Roald Amundsen on his first expedition through the Northwest Passage. The Extreme North was assigned female attributes. For Amundsen, one of the first people to make it to the North Pole, it was the epitome of a sleeping beauty. "Inviting and attractive the fair one lies before us," he wrote. "Yes, we hear you calling, and we shall come. You shall have your kiss, if we pay for it with our lives." Conversely, journeying to the North symbolized a revival of masculinity and a reaction to and rejection of the supposed decadence spreading through Western societies at the fin de siècle.

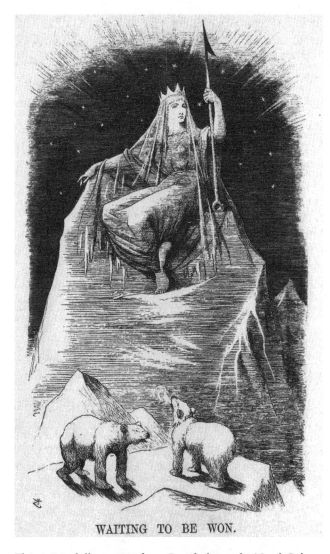

WAITING TO BE WON.

This satirical illustration from *Punch* shows the North Pole as a symbol of femininity. *From* Punch, or the London Chirivari, *June 5, 1875*

When asked in an 1892 interview what he associated with the Arctic, Fridtjof Nansen, who traveled from one end of Greenland to the other and back again, replied: "I think of the Arctic summer rain. I think of the sunshine, reflected from mountains of snow and ice, shining upon little lakes of clear, rippling water, where hundreds of seals playfully splash the water into glistening sprays of rainbow hues. What is the charm of the Arctic? Health, glorious health! Your muscles twitch with a desire for action. You eat like a horse, and sleep twelve or fourteen hours without a dream. Before you is the vast unknown: all around you is silence and solitude." Nansen would frequently refer back to these ideas. In his book *Farthest North* (1897), he reviewed early depictions of the Arctic, including statements by predecessors such as Elisha Kent Kane's assertion "that an Arctic night and Arctic day age a man more rapidly and harshly than a year anywhere else in this weary world." As Nansen correctly pointed out, this reflected Kane's completely inadequate preparations and equipment. With reference to himself, he wrote, "I have not noticed any aging or weakening influence of the polar night in any direction." On the contrary, he felt younger after his Arctic visits. "I would rather recommend these regions as a perfect sanatorium for nervous and weakened people." The simple life of the people he encountered in the North seemed to Nansen to hold the key to human happiness.

In 1909, Robert E. Peary and Fredrick Cook both claimed to have been the first person to travel to the North Pole, with Cook presenting evidence that he had preceded Peary by a year. Accusations flew and the tone turned incendiary. Peary called Cook a "son of a cur," and Cook claimed Peary would stop at nothing, not even murder, to bolster his reputation. Satirical Austrian writer Karl Kraus, the editor of the magazine *Die Fackel* (The Torch), mocked the feud, whose true cause, he felt, were the irrational passions Earth's two poles were capable of inflaming: "For centuries mankind had lacked a final something to satisfy it as it constantly marched forward. What was it? What feverishly occupied people's days and dreams? What captivated a world whose pulse was counted in records? What was the paradigm of all desire? The pinnacle of ambition? The Ultima Thule of curiosity? The substitute for paradise lost? The great sausage being pursued by all sledge dogs at the earthly fair of science? Humanity could not stand the intolerable thought that, somewhere up there, there were a few square miles of land never trodden by the human foot."

Although Kraus thought it inevitable that the poles would be explored, he considered the endeavor entirely senseless. For him, the North was no longer a source of inspiration. The world had been turned upside down, and the pole's "good reputation" had been destroyed by all the feuding. In an essay entitled "The Discovery of the North Pole" from September 1909, he wrote: "Science will make one last attempt and send out its arbiters. Hopefully they will establish that there really is a North Pole because they know it from hearsay. And the Pole will be relieved if it emerges from the affair intact, this self-satisfied spot, 'in relation to which everywhere is south,'— this spot completely subsumed by baseness and without joy since it first came into contact with things human."

An African American explorer from Maryland, born of sharecropper parents before the Civil War, Matthew A. Henson had an eighteen-year partnership in Arctic exploration with Robert Peary. Originally hired as Peary's aide on a seagoing voyage, Henson became the front man on the Artic expeditions, fluent in one Inuit language and an expert dogsled driver, credited for training dog teams in the Inuit way. He was commonly known as "Matthew the Kind One." Much of the success in their expeditions was due to his merit. After they reached the North Pole, Peary—who had always paid Henson minimal wages—not only took possession of Henson's photographs, but refused to recognize his companion's importance to the expedition. What exactly had happened on April, 6 1909? "I was in the lead that had overshot the mark by a couple of miles . . . and I could see that my footprints were the first at the spot," Henson told a newspaper. While Peary, the public face of the expedition, was celebrated as the first at the North Pole, Henson is likely to have been the first man at the top of the world. (Three Inuit members of the crew—Ooqueah, Seegloo, and Egigingwah—also reached the North Pole or came very close to it.) "From the time we knew we were at the Pole, Commander Peary scarcely spoke to me," Henson said later. In 1912, Henson published a book about his experiences, *A Negro Explorer at the North Pole*, and (though it took thirty more years) was the first African American to be made a member (and, a decade later, in 1949, an honorary member) of the eminent Explorers Club of New

Matthew Henson accompanied
Robert Peary on seven trips to
the Arctic. It took a long time
until his contribution received
the recognition it deserved.

Henson, Matthew Alexander, 1866–1955,

courtesy of Library of Congress

York. In 1954, he was invited by President Eisenhower to receive a special
commendation for his work.

Henson is not the only noteworthy companion of Peary who has been
overlooked all too often. Josephine Peary accompanied her husband on six
trips and established a high profile as an Arctic explorer; in fact, she bears
the celebrity title "First Lady of the Arctic." She thus represents a rare
exception on the male-dominated landscape of Arctic endeavor. During
the trips, Ms. Peary prepared food and took care of household chores,
responsibilities she divided with Matthew Henson whenever he was not
needed outside. She also bartered trade goods with the Inuit and is known
to have shared with Inuit women the task of designing and sewing sleeping
bags and clothing from furs. However, "as Josephine upheld the race-based
perspectives typical to her time, she barely tolerated the presence of these
other women," writes anthropological researcher Patricia Pierce Erikson. During the second expedition to Greenland in 1893, Ms. Peary gave
birth to her daughter Marie Ahnighito, called "the snow baby."

Henson, Cook, and Peary notwithstanding, the first time the North Pole
was definitely reached was on May 12, 1926, when the Italian Umberto

Nobile, the Norwegian Roald Amundsen, and the American Lincoln Ells-worth flew over it in their dirigible, the *Norge*. Then, improbably, some thirty years after the first documented human presence at the North Pole, "Thule"—that mythic prehistoric island conceived by the Greeks at least four hundred years before Christ—finally was given a clearly defined geographical location.

It came about like this: Danish polar researcher Knud Rasmussen, who had grown up bilingually with Greenlandic and Danish, was convinced that this legendary land had to be located where people he called the "polar Eskimos" lived. He found them in 1903 on Cape York on the northwest coast of Greenland. Although Rasmussen cast himself rather grandiosely as the discoverer of a previous unknown group of people, there is docu-mented evidence of earlier encounters between Europeans and Indigenous people in this remote region. Rasmussen wrote: "Never in my life have I felt myself to be in such a wild, unaccustomed surroundings, never so far, so very far from home, as when I stood in the midst of the tribe of noisy Polar Eskimos on the beach of Agpat." Rasmussen romantically depicted them as living "outside of any law" as primeval, wholly natural people and urged the Danish government to take a greater interest in the region, noting that Norwegians and Americans were beginning to lay claim to it.

In August 1910, after founding a Thule committee to raise the necessary funds, Rasmussen was able to establish the Cape York Station, Thule. The northernmost human settlement, planned as a base for future trade and research, was a success, and in 1937, four years after Rasmussen's death, Denmark officially assumed its administration. Then, in 1951, political reality interceded, and its fifty-one residents were resettled in Qaanaaq to make way for the US Thule Airbase. The residents resisted their involun-tary relocation and demanded compensation, but their legal arguments, which went all the way to the European Court of Human Rights, were rejected. The North Pole's neighbors—as Rasmussen had called residents of this area—were no longer allowed to live there. On the other hand, Qaanaag, in the northwestern part of Greenland, was officially renamed Thule. After centuries, Ultima Thule was no longer a topological dream.

The Fin de Siècle

Great Expanses and Wind!

Around the turn of the twentieth century the "Northland" put a great many people under its spell. Europeans had come to appreciate the beauty of its wild landscapes, educated audiences were reading the Old Norse sagas, a wave of Celtophilia took hold, and the Vikings were viewed with increased regard. Germany, which had coalesced relatively late as a nation-state, especially connected the North with an urgent search for cultural identity. It was not just a few isolated dreamers who felt that their time had run out and that they no longer optimistically believed in human progress. Not for the first time, the North represented the chance for a profound reorientation. But in contrast to the late eighteenth century, a hundred years before, it was not just the cultural elite turning away from classical Greco-Roman heritage, but a much broader populace, including the bourgeoisie. It combined with a pessimism that was particularly widespread in the German cultural sphere, where Kaiser Wilhelm II's dismissal of the father of German political unity, Otto von Bismarck, represented a rupture many found hard to overcome.

The idea of the North elicited a particular resonance among ethnically chauvinistic and hypernationalist groups in German fraternities, the Munich Cosmic Circle, and the Wagner Society in Bayreuth, the latter led by Cosima and Winifred Wagner and Houston Stewart Chamberlain, who admired the heroes of Norse mythology as role models. A major intellectual predecessor of this movement was Paul Anton Bötticher, alias Paul de Lagarde. Inspired by a deep-seated discomfort with modernity, Lagarde envisioned a Christian-Germanic national religion he believed was rooted in the forests and swamps of northern Europe and preserved in rural communities. Fidus, a pseudonym for Hugo Höppener, one of the most widely known German painters of the fin de siècle associated with the mystical religion of Theosophy, was inspired by the "Northland" to create portraits of heroically lit, blond superhumans. He took his cue from physician, painter, and writer Carl Gustav Carus, for whom Northlanders were "people of the day" and who proposed that the blond hair and blue eyes of many Europeans were directly connected to the sun and sky.

In this context, it's tempting to invoke Friedrich Nietzsche, fascinated as he was by vitality and creative power, and his concept of the "blond beast," but Nietzsche most likely didn't use the phrase in any primary way to describe the northern peoples; rather it designated literally the mane of the lion and figuratively a personality with strong values. "It seems that their Catholicism is much more an intrinsic part of the Latin races than the whole of Christianity in general is of us northerners," Nietzsche wrote. "We northerners are undoubtedly descended from barbarian races also in respect of our talent for religion: we have little talent for it." He also quoted an "old Scandinavian Saga" as saying, "Wotan placed a hard heart in my breast." Nietzsche never drew explicit parallels between any Germanic master race (a notion he rejected) and the heroes of the sagas, although that didn't prevent much of his audience from reading him as though he had. Beyond any doubt is the fact that Nietzsche's cultural pessimism caught on among many people and that the Nazis later falsely claimed him as an intellectual predecessor. It is equally clear that Nietzsche was drawn far more powerfully to the South than to the North. During an 1876 stay in Sorrento, on the Bay of Naples, Italy, where he met Richard Wagner, he wrote in his notebooks: "I don't have enough strength for the North: awkward and artificial souls reign there, who work as constantly and necessarily at the measure of prudence as the beaver at his dam. . . . I have enough spirit for the South."

More popular authors had none of Nietzsche's subtlety and ambiguity. They openly and unapologetically mythologized the North. The ornate *Book of the Northern Land*, published in 1909 by composer Walter Niemann, purported to be an "introduction to the entirety of northern nature and culture." Niemann generously included the Orkney and Shetland Islands and, voicing a widespread prejudice at the time, the Danish colony of Greenland "despite the Mongolian origins of its Eskimo population"— a blatantly racist hypothesis to say the least. Niemann cited his hopes for a romantic transfiguration of the North in Denmark. "The light colors of its landscape, its brighter summer nights, its mutedly hued magic at dusk, its sunrises, in short the entire northern atmosphere," which reminded Niemann of landscapes in central England, made Denmark superior to northern Germany.

He also recognized a more intensive sensibility for nature among the "North Germanics" than among the "Germanics." Apparently influenced by Old Norse popular mythology, Niemann depicted a whole series of natural spirits in his works: good spirits like Tom Thumb, Nisse, water sprites, and elves came from southern Norway and the rest of Scandinavia, while the evil ones hailed from farther north. The composer-author couldn't resist the temptation to try to sum up the essence of Scandinavian authors as a whole. It was a hopeless endeavor, since they came from very different aesthetic schools and, no matter what Niemann's approach, couldn't be reduced to any common denominator. Nonetheless, this enthusiastic admirer of the North expressed his hope that his book would serve the "promotion and convalescence of a good portion of the culture of our German people." Holding Niemann's work in one's hands today, one can imagine the sublimity readers must have felt when they imagined themselves a part of the long, great history of the Scandinavian cultural realm and part of the future project to restore it.

Other authors found less pathos-strained reasons to look northward. Austrian poet Rainer Maria Rilke aligned himself with Scandinavian literature, in which modernism was already more prevalent than in that of many other countries. Among the authors he looked to for direction was Denmark's Jens Peter Jacobsen, whose novelistic protagonist Niels Lyhne was a sensitive poet struggling to balance realism and romanticism. Rilke also admired Sweden's Selma Lagerlöf and August Strindberg, Norways's Henrik Ibsen, Bjørnstjerne Bjørnson, and Knut Hamsun, and Denmark's Herman Bang, all of whom represented new literary currents, even if, like Hamsun, they were not invariably progressives. An extended stay in the artists' colony in Worpswede, in northern Germany, had introduced Rilke, more or less by accident, to the North and its landscapes, and he subsequently taught himself Danish. Books by Scandinavian authors gave him a sense of their attitudes toward life, which he considered the essence of everything future oriented and modern.

Carefully weighing his words, from Germany Rilke wrote to the Swedish women's rights activist and author Ellen Key, who had invited him to Borgeby, in southern Sweden, in 1904: "I believe, although Italy would also do well, that we will soon need the North, great expanses and wind again! It is sad for us to see this quick, overabundant, racing spring, which represents continual decay and consumption by flame, and we long completely for the slow, hesitant arrival of Nordic spring days, the great and portentous transformations of Nordic nature, in whose existence every little flower is a life, a world, a beginning, a destiny: quite a lot. What is a little flower here, where there are millions of blossoms!"

Not all of Rilke's contemporaries expressed their admiration for the North so poetically. "I am of a Nordic mind, with the complete certainty that today obtains everywhere on matters of nationality and race," wrote an uncharacteristically emphatic Thomas Mann in an answer to a 1904 questionnaire. "Protestant, moral, Puritanical leanings—who knows where they come from?—inhabit my blood." Statements like this were presaged in Mann's 1903 novella *Tonio Kröger*: "Italy is of no interest at all to me—I almost despise it . . . I can't stand all those terribly lively people down there with their dark animal way of looking at you . . . I'm taking a short trip to Denmark . . . I must have gotten this Nordic inclination from my father, since my mother was actually more one for the *bellezza*, inasmuch as she cared for anything at all. Think of the books written up there, those profoundly lucid books full of good humor—there's nothing better, I just love them. Think of the Scandinavian cuisine, that incomparable cuisine, which can only be taken in strong salt air . . . Think of the names they have! They're like adornments—many of them were also common where I'm from. Think of a name like 'Ingeborg'—it's like three notes plucked on harp strings, it's pure poetry. And then there's the sea—they have the Baltic Sea up there!"

By contrast, nativist authors like Ludwig Ganghofer, Peter Rosegger, and Hermann Löns categorically rejected intellectual literature and openly worshipped everything rural and agrarian, rhapsodizing about the "preeminence of blond blood." "I'm proud of the fact," wrote Löns, who was best known for his nature poetry about the romantic Lüneburg Heath landscape in northern Germany, in 1912, "that you don't need to think to read my books."

Kaiser Wilhelm II was still making his annual voyages to Scandinavia—and tourists followed in his footsteps—well into the Weimar Republic. But in the summer of 1914, a crisis intervened. A group of Americans, English, French, and Russians boarded the luxury steamship *Prinz Friedrich Wilhelm* bound for Norway in anticipation of encountering the German monarch, who, as every year, was planning to meet his friend, the painter Hans Dahl, in Balestrand, on the northern bank of the Sognefjord. But on August 14, the traveling party received word of the outbreak of the First World War. Not only did they have to abandon their dreams of a royal encounter; the jovial atmosphere and newly made friendships were abruptly over. Their ship reached Norway but was no longer able to sail back to Germany. All the passengers had to arrange transportation back home on their own. The kaiser, of course, had long since returned to Germany.

Developing Nordic Proclivities Further

The image of Thor swinging his hammer would get a second life of sorts during the First World War in French anti-German propaganda, in which it was used as a cypher for vicious Germans—indeed, murderous Huns. "The god Thor, the most barbaric among the barbaric divinities of old Germania," read the subtitle of an image widely distributed in Paris in 1915. Such images and ideas were part of the French reaction to the militarism of the kaiser and Germany's invasion of Belgium and northern France.

"Nordic proclivities" continued to be stoked by writings aimed at exploiting the public tastes of the times. Starting in 1911, Eugen Diederichs began to publish the *Thule Collection*, intended to be a twenty-four-volume compendium of Old Norse texts covering everything from the *Edda* to the sagas. The first volume of this Old Icelandic library—Diederichs had been able to enlist a number of scholars as editors—contained "The Story of the Skald Egil," a Viking-era saga of war. Diedrichs had no scruples about incorrectly asserting that the ancient writings had been preserved, with no later amendment or changes, from heathen days. "Thule is not the past," read the publishing houses catalog, "Thule is the eternal Germanic soul." The final volume of the *Thule Collection* appeared in 1930, the year of Diedrich's death. A copy was sent to Reykjavík for Iceland's millennial celebrations.

In his epochal work *The Decline of the West* (1918), the German philosopher of history Oswald Spengler didn't lionize the North to the extent of many of his contemporaries, but he nonetheless gave a decisive role in the course of world history to the people who lived there, writing that the "old Northern races, in whose primitive souls the Faustian [spirit] was already awakening, discovered in their grey dawn the art of sailing the seas which emancipated them. The Egyptians knew the sail, but only profited by it as a labor-saving device. They sailed, as they had done before in their oared ships, along the coast to Punt and Syria, but the idea of the high-seas voyage—what it meant as a liberation, a symbol—was not in them."

"Because of an internal reason," Spengler wrote, the men of antiquity could not become conquerors, and "the Romans made no attempt to penetrate the interior of Africa." The people of the North were the opposite: "The never-stilled desire to be liberated from the binding element, to range far and free, which is the essence of the fancy-creatures of the North—the dwarfs, elves and imps—is utterly unknown to the Dryads and Oreads of Greece. . . . . To settle far from the coast would have meant to lose sight of 'home,' while to settle in loneliness—the ideal life of the trapper and prairie-man of America as it had been of Icelandic saga-heroes long before—was something entirely beyond the possibilities of classical mankind. Dramas like that of the emigration to America—man by man, each on his own account, driven by deep promptings to loneliness—or the Spanish Conquest, or the Californian gold-rush, dramas of uncontrollable longings for freedom, solitude, immense independence, and of giantlike contempt of all limitations whatsoever upon the home-feeling—these dramas are Faustian and only Faustian. No other Culture, not even the Chinese, knows them."

It was hardly an accident that the secret, ethnically chauvinist Thule Society was established in Germany in 1918. Its founder, Rudolf von Sebottendorf, a devotee of mystical writings, was able to attract fifteen hundred members in the association's heyday, including the later chief Nazi ideologue Alfred Rosenberg and Hitler's later deputy Rudolf Hess. Along with spreading vitriolic anti-Semitic and anti-Bolshevik propaganda, the society sought to topple the postwar People's Free State of Bavaria and somewhat later the short-lived Bavarian Soviet Republic, whose military police stormed the Four Seasons Hotel in Munich in April 1919, detaining society members and executing a number of them.

It was the same year that saw the death of occult Austrian author Guido von List, who, after intensely studying runic inscriptions, came to believe that they held magic powers. List had suffered from temporary blindness and thought the visions he developed during this time revealed the hidden meanings of the *Edda* and the Old Germanic symbols. He also thought that blond and blue-eyed "Aryans" had originated from a continent at the North Pole and were forced south by the Ice Age, where they brought culture to all of humanity and mixed with the southern races. List's idea of a "Pan-Germany" encompassed Germans, English, Dutch, Danes, Swedes, and Norwegians, whom he wanted to unite against the Jews, whom he considered "hostile nomads." His doctrine of wotanism, an ethnically chauvinistic brand of mysticism named after the Germanic god Wotan, invoked the *Edda*, and in a variety of indirect ways, he influenced the symbolism later used by Hitler's SS. As Brigitte Hamann writes in *Hitler's Vienna* (1999), her detailed exploration of the early development of Hitler's worldview, the führer in waiting referenced List's ideas about the swastika in one of his speeches at the Munich Hofbräuhaus (a popular beer hall). "Aryans" had brought "the sign of the sun," Hitler told his followers, to the ice-cold North: "They build all their cults around light and they find the sign, the tool for lighting a fire, the whisk, the cross. . . . It is the swastika of the communities once founded by Aryan culture." Hitler also echoed List's ideas at another point in the speech: "We know that Egypt reached its high cultural level on account of Aryan immigrants, as did Persia and Greece; the immigrants were blond, blue-eyed Aryans, and we know for a fact that no cultural nation has been founded on earth except for those countries. To be sure, there were mixed races in between the black, dark-eyed and dark-skinned southern race and the immigrants of the northern race, but there were no great independent, creative cultural nations."

People in Germany continued to glorify the North, reaching higher and higher levels of hyperbole. This may not have been inevitable, but in retrospect, the ground for such a valorization had been sowed for quite some time. Enthusiasm for the North was not just part of the circles around the kaiser but in the entire "Wandervogel" (Wandering Bird) hiking movement, which had discovered a new primeval landscape, along with the Alps, to explore. And then there was the light in the North: Scandinavia was seen predominantly as the realm of the midnight sun and bright light. The dark days and long nights of winter that weighed so heavily on the first European travelers to the region were no longer mentioned.

Swedish painter Carl Larsson was second to none in depicting this pastel-colored world, flooded with joy. (He had honed his preference for watercolors during his years in France.) The idea of an abstract Nordic landscape, which had coalesced among the German back-to-nature movement at the turn of the century, was supplemented by customs supposedly reminiscent of heathen practices, such as extended celebrations of the solstice. These practices were inspired by the Swedish *midsommar* or Denmark's equivalent *Sankt Hans Aften* that traditionally featured huge bonfires in central places or near or even on lake platforms—to be more easily seen from afar. The ritual followed set procedures and ended with crosses being thrown on the fire to commemorate the dead. The leaders of the Hitler Youth, the organization of the Nazi Party in Germany for male youth between the ages of 14 and 18, concocted similar ceremonies based on these customs, which were adapted to the purpose of strengthening dedication to the führer ("leader," meaning Hitler). These included, among others, the reciting of verses, the celebration of youth consecration as rite of passage, and "mock funerals" for "fallen comrades."

In 1925, Austrian author Stefan Zweig recalled: "Germany's best and indeed all of the creative literature of the fin de siècle became enthralled by the magic of the North. Scandinavia meant to that generation what Russia did to earlier ones and Far East perhaps today: a new country of the soul, a primeval source of unsuspected problems. Back then, Ibsen, Bjørnson and Strindberg seemed so primally powerful, so revolutionary, so disruptive to that generation as Dostoyevsky and Tolstoy are today for the European soul. . . . This literary wave blew in like a massive gust of wind, free, intellectual wind. A very great Germanic tribe had broken in upon German literature like in the days of the migration of peoples. It was a mighty, triumphant phalanx, of whom today the intellectual leader Georg Brandes and the late arrival and last of the *triarii* Knut Hamsun still occupy space within the boundaries of our intellectual life. The din of all these battles has subsided in the meantime, and today we no longer fully understand these once so stormily won victories."

After Strindberg and Ibsen, Hamsun became the best-known Scandinavian writer in Europe in the first decade of the twentieth century, someone to whom Zweig ascribed "the noblest form of masculinity, namely tenderness, which bubbles up with the great strength; passion, which conceals itself behind severe acridity." With Hamsun's 1890 novel *Hunger*, a book about a person torn apart by ambivalent conflicts, who starves himself in devotion to literary accomplishment, Hamsun liberated himself from the familiar traditions of the novel. Across Europe, *Hunger* was regarded as groundbreaking in style. Motifs from it recur in the works of Kafka and Beckett. James Joyce was electrified by it and learned Norwegian to be able to read it in the original language. In 1920, Hamsun won the Nobel Prize in Literature. Ernest Hemingway and Henry Miller were among his admirers. Hamsun, who had lived in Wisconsin and Minnesota during the 1880s, rejected both Communist and Anglo-American capitalist societies. He became a key figure in Norwegian nationalism, was known as a long-time admirer of Germany, later developed clear sympathies for Hitler, and acted as a collaborator during Germany's occupation of Norway. Indeed, he gave his Nobel medal to Joseph Goebbels and visited Adolf Hitler at the German leader's mountain retreat, Berghof in Obersalzberg, in Upper Bavaria.

The Abyss of
"Racial Science"

Germany was still reeling from the catastrophe of the First World War when linguist Hans Friedrich Karl Günther published his study *Racial Science of the German People* in 1922. Günther's theories channeled interest in the North in an ominous new direction. Günther was interested in training his readers' awareness of "the form, the image, the palpable-physical essence of appearance," writing: "He who does not immediately register, in the moment of observation, the narrowness or broadness of a head, or does not feel the urge to perceive the arch of an eye, the bend of a nose, the curve of the lips, a particular shape of the chin as a system of lines and surfaces in order to be able to recreate it in his imagination; he who does not immediately note such patterns overlooks an aspect—a significant aspect—of all phenomena."

The goal of his brand of racial science was to describe this "superior" branch of humanity and lay out a plan for its representatives to both survive biologically and maintain or recapture their political and cultural supremacy. The flip side of the agenda was his claim that the vast majority of Europeans were "half-breeds" or "bastards." Günther located the Nordic race in its purest form in one specific place: the region surrounding the Vättern, a lake in Sweden's southern Småland Province.

Günther established a "Nordic movement" whose mission was to increase the share of "Nordic blood" in the population in question— this was what he understood as biological "nordification." The movement was embodied by the Nordic Society, which was founded around 1921 and was initially not affiliated with any political party. The society's headquarters were in the northern German city of Lübeck, with forty-three branches eventually appearing throughout Germany. In addition, liaison officers were installed in Copenhagen, Oslo, Reykjavík, Stockholm, and Helsinki and charged with raising awareness of the "new Germany" among cultural representatives in their respective countries. In Lübeck, not all that far from Scandinavia, the society's members fretted about the downfall of the "Nordic race." The governing principle for these efforts was the "pan-Nordic ideal," essentially an ambitious foreign policy program involving "the unification of the Germanic-language speaking peoples with the goal of Nordic rebirth." According to Günther's classification, the Germans were one of six Nordic peoples alongside the Danes, Icelanders, Norwegians, Swedes, and Finns.

Günther's idea of "nordification" recalls a project of Willibald Hentschel, an anti-Semitic proponent of race hygiene who studied biology under Ernst Haeckel, an evolutionary biologist, eugenicist, and Darwin's staunchest champion in Germany, best known for his masterful and often colorful illustrations and prints of various organisms in *Art Forms in Nature* (1899– 1904). At the turn of the twentieth century, Hentschel developed a plan for "race-breeding sites," so-called Mittgard settlements, which would bring one hundred men together with ten times that number of women. It presaged the covert Lebensborn maternity homes set up by the SS for "selective breeding" in various countries before and during the Second World War. Günther didn't go as far as the influential "racial hygienicist" Fritz

Lenz, who dreamed of both a "Blond Internationale" and a confederation of all "European civilized" peoples. Lenz was part of a tradition of authors propagating the cult of blondness.

In 1923, Günther moved to Scandinavia with his Norwegian wife, Maggen Blom, first to the Norwegian province of Telemark and later to the city of Uppsala, in Sweden. The Swedish Institute for Race Biology, a government research institute—the first of its kind worldwide—had been founded there the previous year with the aim of studying eugenics and genetics, and they occasionally employed Günther as a researcher. When he returned to Germany six years later, he was soon awarded a post as a professor for social anthropology at the University of Jena, Thuringia. On the day of his inaugural lecture, the hall was overflowing with guests, including Hitler.

Over the years, Günther revised *Racial Science of the German People*, influenced by collaborators from Germany and beyond. Swedish author Rolf Nordenstreng, for example, contributed details about the "physical and psychological traits" of the "East Baltic race." Günther went on to document his religious and ideological worldview in *Piety of the Nordic Strain* (1934), a book that had no compunctions about enlisting William Shakespeare, the archaeologist and art historian Johann Joachim Winckelmann, and the poet Friedrich Hölderlin as supposed proponents of his brand of Aryan-Nordic spirituality.

A series of books in the English-speaking world had already covered similar terrain as Günther's. One was *The Passing of the Great Race; or, The Racial Basis of European History*, published in the United States in 1916 and still one of the most famous and notorious racist texts ever. Its author, Madison Grant, a graduate of Yale and Columbia Universities, was the scion of a wealthy New York family who could afford to devote himself to his racial obsessions. Grant, otherwise known for his efforts to save endangered species from extinction, promoted the "Nordic race" as superior and responsible for Western civilization's greatest achievements. His book discussed the geographical migration of peoples and "races" and glorified light-skin and blond hair. In Grant's view, the "great race" had origi-

DER N⊕RDEN

MONATSSCHRIFT DER NORDISCHEN GESELLSCHAFT

NR. 9 21. JAHRGANG SEPTEMBER 1944 PREIS 85 RPF. · WILHELM LIMPERT-VERLAG, BERLIN SW 68
A. MAHLAU

The Nordic Society often used Scandinavian folkloristic patterns (here a bridal shawl) for the covers of their magazine, *Der Norden*—issue September 1944. *Courtesy of Wolfgang Horner*

nated in the forests and plains of eastern Germany, Poland, and Russia. He also advanced the strange notion that Leonardo da Vinci, Michelangelo, and Dante must have had "Nordic blood."

Franz Boas reviewed this tract in an article for *The New Republic* entitled "Nordic Propaganda," criticizing Grant as "dangerous," "dogmatic," and "naive." Grant responded that he was not surprised by such a reaction from a member of "inferior races"—Boas was Jewish.

The publication of Grant's book coincided with the rebirth of the Ku Klux Klan and its message of hatred for Blacks, Jews, and Catholics. As the Klan unleashed a campaign of terror and lynching in the American South, millions of people were purchasing Grant's best-selling book. Grant went on to be the main proponent of the eugenics movement in the United States, directing the Working Committee of the Eugenics Research Association from 1916 on. On this issue Grant wrote: "Mistaken regard for what are believed to be divine laws and a sentimental belief in the sanctity of human life tend to prevent both the elimination of defective infants and the sterilization of such adults as are themselves of no value to the community. The laws of nature require the obliteration of the unfit and human life is valuable only when it is of use to the community or race." Crazy as they may seem today, Grant's ideas were hardly fringe opinions in the political discourse of his day. In 1916, Teddy Roosevelt commented: "The book is a capital book; in purpose, in vision, in grasp of the facts our people most need to realize. It shows an extraordinary range of reading and a wide scholarship. It shows a habit of singular serious thought on the subject of most commanding importance. It shows a fine fearlessness in assailing the popular and mischievous sentimentalities and attractive and corroding falsehoods which few men dare assail." Calvin Coolidge wrote in 1921 in *Good Housekeeping*: "The Nordics propagate themselves successfully. With other races, the outcome shows deterioration on both sides. Quality of mind and body suggests that observance of ethnic law is as great a necessity to a nation as immigration law."

Grant played a key role in the passage of laws limiting immigration from eastern Europe and Asia, and for a time he served as vice president of the Immigration Restriction League. And while Albert Johnson, a Republican from Washington State and chief author of the Immigration Act, also an anti-Semite, supported many of Grant's positions, he took a decidedly different stance on the House floor in April 1924: "As regards the charge . . . that this committee has started out deliberately to establish a blond race . . . let me say that such a charge is all in your eye. Your committee is not the author of any of these books on the so-called Nordic race."

Grant's book was translated and published in German in 1925, paving the way for his popularity among the Nazis, although the exact influence is difficult to measure. The book was appreciated for his racist ideas. Or criticized for them. The Austrian anthropologist Viktor Lebzelter reviewed the book for the magazine *Anthropos* in 1926: "This work is scientifically meaningless and is meant simply as academic propaganda for Grant the politician. It has been translated to illustrate to the German readership that people in America put forth some of the same ideas advanced in German by some literati and politically active scholars. The book was translated by the professor of dermatology and syphilidology Dr. Rudolf Polland in Graz. In the context of this magazine . . . I need cite but a single remark concerning the black race: 'The stoppage of famines and wars and the abolition of the slave trade, while dictated by the noblest impulses of humanity, are suicidal to the white man. Upon the removal of these natural checks Negroes multiply so rapidly that there will not be standing room on the continent for white men, unless, perchance, the lethal sleeping sickness, which attacks the natives far more frequently than the whites, should run its course unchecked.' In his defense we can only say that as a lawyer, Mr. Grant obviously doesn't know what sleeping sickness is."

Adolf Hitler was an enthusiastic reader of Grant's pseudoscientific opus and wrote to Grant in the early 1930s, declaring, "It is my Bible." Apparently unaware of who exactly his German fan was, Grant sent him a signed copy. This volume is kept in the Library of Congress in Washington, DC, after American soldiers found it in 1945 among the books in Hitler's mountain retreat near Berchtesgaden. Hitler quoted Grant both in *Mein Kampf* and in various speeches. When he was interviewed by the *New York Times* in 1932, Hitler said: "It was America that taught us a nation should not open its doors equally to all nations."

The Nordic Society, placed under Nazi control in 1933 and awarded "seals of honor," organized "Nordic weeks" and "Northland voyages"— although the ships often simply sailed along the coast to prevent having to exchange currency. The real purpose of these trips was indoctrination, to make the passengers feel that they were part of a mission to strengthen their bonds with their northern European "brethren." In July 1936, for example, 620 passengers boarded the *Milwaukee*. The itinerary was described as follows: "The trip went from Hamburg to the Faroe Islands and from there to Iceland, then on to Bergen and the Norwegian coast back to the starting point. In the bay by Reykjavík a reception was held on board the Milwaukee for public figures in Iceland. Halfway to Norway, the passengers enjoyed a beer festival, and a 'Hanseatic evening' with Norwegian guests took place in Bergen."

No matter how cozy such descriptions may sound, the relationship between Germany and "North Germania," as the Nazis sometimes called Scandinavia, was anything but harmonious. As early as 1934, Rosenberg voiced frustration with the northern neighbors. "Scandinavia has had it too good, it has gotten overfed and lazy," he complained in one of his diary entries. "The Vikings emigrated and the burghers stayed behind. It will take a hard blow to stir the old blood to rebellion once more."

One passenger of a Northland voyage was Bernhard Kummer, a German academic nicknamed "Germanic Bernhard" for his expertise in Old Norse languages. He was critical of what he experienced. "One senses, especially in Reykjavík, something of the country's Europeanization or its Americanization," he wrote. "We do not tolerate such internationalization." And the race psychologist Eberhard Dannheim lamented that Reykjavík resembled "an American Gold Rush town"—a misfortune he blamed on the Icelandic tradespeople's "unsound business practices." He also had harsh words for the Icelanders' supposedly unrealistic expectations for the future, their "craving of intoxication," the "typical examples of bohemians who care little about their appearance," and the "sexual permissiveness" he claimed often took the form of adultery. A particular thorn in his eye—along with the "impertinent children"—was the extent to which the sexes enjoyed equal rights. "The Icelandic woman takes the liberty of making decisions for herself whether she is married or not," he carped. German propaganda about the traditional role of women must have seemed bizarre in Scandinavia. The ideological and political differences between the countries were simply irreconcilable. Swedes passionately defended ideals like freedom of expression, a free nation under the rule of law, and tolerance toward those with different views. Although several leading representatives of racial theory came from Sweden, they did not subscribe to the version of it that was so loudly propagated and instrumentalized as an ideology in Germany.

The touristic interest of Germans in Scandinavia and beyond was actively promoted not only by the Nordic Society, but also by tourist organizations in Denmark, Sweden, and Norway. Interestingly, the tourist association of Denmark, to give one example, seems to have been very well aware of the ideological proclivities of their potential visitors: their 1936 English-language brochure, geared toward visitors from Britain, mentions that Denmark entertains "the most advanced social laws of the world." That line does not appear in the German-language version.

The Scandinavian countries competed with Italy as a tourist destination. The latter's relative geographical proximity, the continued role of Latin classics in university education, the popularity of Italian music, and the beguiling travels recorded by Johann Wolfgang von Goethe in his *Italian Journey* all contributed to an almost mythological longing for the South. In the 1930s, Italy also served an ideological purpose for the Nazi leadership: "As a kind of touristic counterpart to a diplomatic alliance, travel to Italy was promoted as a way to unite the two fascist countries. Commercial tourism publicity and KdF [*Kraft durch Freude*— Strength through Joy, the Nazi leisure organization] literature alike praised the Italian government and included new buildings and other sites associated with Mussolini and his Blackshirts within their itineraries," writes Kristin Semmens in *Seeing Hitler's Germany: Tourism in the Third Reich*. Spain, Portugal, and Greece—other countries in the fascist orbit— were also recommended.

The Nazis were offended when the Nobel Committee of the Norwegian parliament awarded the 1935 Nobel Peace Prize to the German dissident Carl von Ossietzky. Four years earlier, the pacifist author had been sentenced to prison for publications considered treasonous. Detained in 1932, he was later released but was rearrested in 1933 and confined in a concentration camp until May of 1936. Knut Hamsun, Sven Hedin, and even the

In the 1930s, the Norwegian tourist industry used idealized "Nordics" for their campaigns. *Courtesy of Norsk Jernbanemuseum*

heirs of Alfred Nobel himself all publicly opposed the choice of Ossietzky for the honor.

While at this point barely anyone in the English-speaking countries was particularly interested in the origin of the Nordic peoples, many people in Germany definitely were. In his 1922 work *Atlantis, the Original Homeland of the Aryans,* German author Karl Georg Zschaetzsch claimed to have located the legendary island off the Spanish and Moroccan coasts: "The original homeland of the blond, blue-eyed Aryan tribe, also known to us generally as the Germanic people, was the island of Atlantis, which disappeared into the sea as a result of the catastrophe known as the Flood. Its remnants still rise above the Atlantic Ocean in the form of the Azores."

But social scientist Herman Wirth, a Dutchman who worked in Germany, claimed that the Nordic population had originated in the polar region. His 1928 book *The Emergence of Mankind* describes how these people had evolved from apes in the Far North several million years in the past and been driven southward five hundred thousand years ago through a series of ice ages. Wirth believed that the blond Eskimos discovered by Denmark's Thule expedition, led by Knut Rasmussen at the beginning of the twentieth century, were actually the remnants of this "Atlantean-Nordic" race. He also believed that these Arctic people had lived in a matriarchal social system governed by a "great Mother." Zschaetzsch drew on a wide variety of utterly unrelated texts, including the *Edda*, to link Atlantis with Hercules, Thor, Indra, and the Inca king Inti-Kapak.

Alfred Rosenberg, who was born in Estonia, which was part of Russia at the time, propagated equally obscure "truths." Rosenberg claimed to have located the original home of the Germanic tribes—a group he conflated with the Indo-Germanic peoples—in northern Europe, ignoring what had become the accepted theory that the latter had migrated to Europe from farther east. He also considered Jesus Christ to be the "personification of the Nordic racial soul" and therefore by definition not Jewish, and saw Germany, not Palestine, as the real "Holy Land." In his opinion, even Ahura Mazda, the Persian god of light and highest deity of Zoroastrianism, must have originated in the High North, while the "Aryan" was engaged in constant battle with the "Jewish demon," "the master of darkness." In his 1930 book *The Myth of the 20th Century*, an esoteric mix of racist mysticism and philosophy, Rosenberg wrote: "It seems far from impossible that in areas over which Atlantic waves roll and giant icebergs float, a flourishing continent once rose above the waters, and upon it a creative race produced a far-reaching culture and sent its children out into the world as seafarers and warriors. But even if this Atlantis hypothesis should prove untenable, a prehistoric Nordic cultural center must still be assumed." At the Institute for German Ancestral Heritage, run by the SS, researchers declared that Heligoland, the small German island outpost in the North Sea, was actually once the capital of Atlantis. (Heligoland first belonged to Denmark, then, from 1807 to 1890, to Britain before it was ceded to Germany. From 1945 to 1952 it belonged to the United Kingdom again, as a war prize.)

Hitler defined the "Aryan" as the "Prometheus of mankind." For him, the term *Nordic* stood for those qualities that, through interaction with the hostile climate, emerged as the highest and most perfect human imaginable. Belonging to the "correct" ethnic group was key: although Laplanders and Eskimos were denizens of the North, Hitler denied them any ability at all to create culture. By this point, the question of the origin of human culture, which had been a subject of intense scientific debate just a few decades earlier, had been declared closed. The speculation that migration from the North drove Europe's cultural advancement became state doctrine in Germany, and the toxic climate of Nazism suffocated opposing views.

Heinrich Himmler, the head of the SS, went even further, dreaming of resurrecting the Nordic religion of the supposed Ur-Aryans. But he was something of an exception. Old Norse texts had little to no cultural influence on the Third Reich for the simple reason that they were difficult to digest. Wagner's work was more popular and comprehensible and thus much easier to co-opt for the Nazis' purposes. Goebbels's Propaganda Ministry used it to package the war as a media spectacle, for example, so that Wagner's "Ride of the Valkyries" achieved the dubious distinction of serving in the weekly newsreels as the soundtrack to footage of the Wehrmacht's 1941 invasion of Crete.

"Aryan" Brothers
in the South

With their militaristic vocabulary and their stereotypes of mortal enemies, the Nazis found like-minded allies in Italy. The 1934 book *Revolt against the Modern World*, by rural Sicilian aristocrat and cultural philosopher Julius Evola, advanced an esoteric theory of Arctic origins involving sun worship and masculine values. But even though Evola's writings were published in Germany, he didn't attract the sympathies of the Nordic movement—in contrast to the enthusiasm that greeted fellow Italian Julius Cogni. That was despite the fact that Cogni distanced himself from anti-Semitism—his focus was on convincing his German readers and intellectual fellow travelers "that Italians have a lot more Nordic blood in them than commonly acknowledged."

Even at the very start of the twentieth century, there were voices advocating a close alliance between Italy and northern Europe. In 1908, Gino Bertolini proposed that "it can only benefit the Italian people if they attach themselves in the long term to the Germanic race not just via the formal bonds of a political alliance but also in terms of lasting intellectual relationships." Bertolini's agenda and goal was, as he put it, "the rebirth of the great Roman people's soul"—an ideal he shared with Mussolini, who came to power in 1922. The Italian fascists were sick of Italians being seen as clichéd ice cream vendors and opera singers. They longed instead for truly heroic role models.

The speculative theories proliferating about "the North" and "the South" possessed an irresistible appeal to those who repeatedly tried to define those concepts. In 1929, Prussian culture minister and Orientalist Carl Heinrich Becker wrote: "The South is what we don't have but desire. The North is very different. We feel the North present deep within our most personal life. We cannot escape it. It lives in our blood, in the mysterious depths of our personality as a people and as individuals. Our creative spirit somehow comes from the south, but the primeval creative power of our soul is of northern origin."

The term *Nordic* used in the racial context goes back to the Russian-French anthropologist Joseph Deniker, chief librarian at the Paris Natural History Museum beginning in 1888. Deniker is known for creating maps of the distribution of "principal and secondary races" across Europe. "Principal races" included Nordic, Littoral/Atlanto-Mediterranean, Oriental, Adriatic/Dinaric, Ibero-Insularic, and Occidental/Cévennic; "secondary races" included Subnordic, North-Occidental, Vistulian, and Subadriatic. The American anthropologist Paul Radin (who had been a student of Franz Boas) wrote in *The Racial Myth* (1934) that the doctrine of Nordic superiority is the "compensated myth of confused late comers, of people whose historical rhythm has not synchronized with that of the rest of the world." Reviewing Radin's book in 1934, the *New York Times* commented: "When Germany threw a much enlarged hat into the ring of the nations and announced that her people are superior to all others because they are Nordics, she struck a fuse that has set off a bombardment of books that by facts, arguments, ridicule, every possible literary means has endeavored to convince her of her error and to show all the rest of the world how immature, mistaken and futile is her assumption."

During the Third Reich, Nazi ideologues looked to the nineteenth century for intellectual predecessors, for instance, by posthumously appropriating early Romantic painter Caspar David Friedrich. Friedrich's landscapes were praised as "coastal art," assigned to the topographic "northern realm," and interpreted as works created from the soul of the "Nordic race." Friedrich's fondness for winter and autumnal scenes, the "Nordic seasons," and for classically "Nordic trees" like oaks and firs fit in well with such interpretations. In 1939, art historian Kurt Karl Eberlein wrote: "The old inheritance of Germanic nature and the Nordic spirit of art glimmering under the ashes was revived once more [in Friedrich]. His soulful art is the art of Northern resistance against all of the South's art of depiction." A testimonial book of the Art Historical Institute at the University of Greifswald stressed Friedrich's "Germanic" fundamental characteristics, expressed in his "Nordic love of light, stone and graves and in his down-to-earth worship of nature." Conversely, an example of an artist who could not be reinterpreted in this way was the painter Ernst Wilhelm Nay, who had been invited to the Lofoten archipelago in Norway by Edvard Munch. His works depicted fisherman and whalers in the modernist style and were rejected by the Nazis and included in the notorious "decadent art" exhibit in Munich in 1937.

Because Nazi ideologues included the ancient Greeks as part of the "Aryan race," there were no obstacles to enlisting them for the cause, especially as National Socialist visions of the ideal human body were borrowed from sculptures of ancient Greek athletes. This logic was extended to include the notions that "Aryans" had founded the antique culture of southern Europe during the migration of peoples and that the Greeks were "Aryan brothers" of the Germans, who were also seen as having come down from the North. In a 1935 proclamation by the Nazi minister for science, education and popular training, Bernhard Rust, this vacuous theory was declared a fact that was henceforth to be promoted without contradiction: "World history is to be presented as the history of racially determined ethnicities. Taking the place of the school of 'ex oriente lux' is the knowledge that at least all of the Occidental cultures—in Asia Minor, Greece, Rome and the rest of the European countries—are primarily the work of Nordic peoples, most of whom prevailed in battle with other races."

The Nazis had no objection to depictions of Italian and Arcadian landscapes, and Roman virtues were proclaimed as German ones as well, since both groups were considered Indo-Germanic. The Germanic tribes were thus no longer the antipode of the Romans, as they had been in previous North-South antitheses. Instead, as the contemporary Scandinavian and Germanic medievalist Klaus von See has shown, the main line of conflict now ran between Germanic people and Jews. It was fitting in this context that Hitler and Mussolini would create the "Berlin-Rome axis" that would hold until 1943. In one of his mealtime monologues, Hitler went off on a lengthy tangent describing the Italian renaissance as the "dawning of a new day and a self-rediscovery of Aryan man."

Scandinavia, Anti-Fascist Bulwark

It was popular to romanticize Scandinavia into a bucolic idyll and to incessantly praise it for its natural beauty since the early nineteenth century, but the region had begun to awaken out of its torpor during the course of the nineteenth century. Even at the turn of the twentieth century, visitors noticed how developed the Scandinavian telephone network was, how reliably trains ran, and how widely available electricity was, even in remote areas. Men and women were even occasionally allowed to bathe together on select beaches! And then there was the progressive nature of the educational system and the fact that Scandinavian writers were discarding outmoded conventions and thematizing the challenges of the new era in their stories and plays. Ibsen's dramas, for example, unleashed scandals in Paris, Barcelona, and elsewhere.

The origins of the Scandinavian countries' markedly collective understanding of society go a long way back. The Scandinavian outlook was scarcely imaginable without Lutheranism. Unlike Calvinism, whose capitalistic ideals greatly influenced other parts of Europe, the Scandinavian Protestant ethic encouraged the social welfare state from early on. It included regard for hard work, equality between men and women, and the principle "Do unto others as you would have them do unto you." Seen thusly, Scandinavian social democracy and its concepts of equality have something of a modern religion.

From early on, women were occasionally able to break into male domains. The Swedish chemist and agrarian scientist Eva Ekeblad was accepted as a member of the Royal Swedish Academy of Sciences in 1748, although she remained the only woman in this elite circle until 1910. Among other things, Ekeblad was famous for discovering how to make alcohol and flour from potatoes, which had been introduced into Sweden a century before.

In the 1890s, this discourse of equality and social equity was extended to the political and academic levels. Sweden's Social Democratic Party was founded in 1889 and was able to govern by majority coalition in the early twentieth century. The central figure was Karl Hjalmar Branting (1860–1925), who led the party for many years and became Sweden's first Social Democratic prime minister.

In the 1930s, with the Social Democrats having cemented their status as the most important force in Swedish politics, there was a push to institute social engineering projects. This would last until the 1970s. Over the decades, Sweden succeeded in finding a balance between high taxes and low inequality, universal social welfare systems and robust economic growth.

Over the course of the 1930s, social scientists from many Western countries began taking an interest in Denmark, Sweden, and Norway as the bearers of a shared value system. These nations had presented themselves as a unified ensemble at the World Fairs since the 1920s. Whether in terms of infrastructure, health care, or education, Scandinavian reform initiatives were everywhere.

Among the Americans who aligned themselves most closely with the

Scandinavian countries was journalist Marquis W. Childs, who worked for three decades for the *St. Louis Post-Dispatch*. He saw the Scandinavian model as a middle course between capitalism and communism that promised to alleviate the negative side effects of both. All the way back in the 1920s, the Rockefeller Foundation financially supported the Social Institute in Stockholm. The American president at the time, Franklin D. Roosevelt, praised Child's 1936 book *Sweden, the Middle Way* and was inspired by the examples and social experiments described therein. "In Sweden, for example, you have a royal family and a Socialist Government and a capitalist system, all working happily side by side," wrote FDR. In 1936, Roosevelt sent a delegation to analyze the cooperative system that a few decades later would become known as the Swedish, Scandinavian, or Nordic model: a social welfare state that included a relatively high level of benefits by international comparison and an intense emphasis on education, among other aspects. Another major figure in this context was Swedish economist Gunnar Myrdal, who was commissioned at the time by the Carnegie Corporation to carry out an interdisciplinary study on ethnic and racial relations in the United States. Together with his wife Alva, he soon began holding regular lectures in America about Scandinavian social welfare policies. In the late 1930s, Sweden and the United States established a joint news agency in the latter to disseminate information about the former.

The results of Myrdal's study included the realization that poverty leads to more poverty as well as the criticism of two policies implemented by Roosevelt that destroyed jobs for hundreds of thousands of African Americans. Published in 1944 as *An American Dilemma: The Negro Problem and American Democracy*, the study had a massive impact and played a not insubstantial role in the Supreme Court's 1954 decision to declare educational segregation unconstitutional. At least in the minds of many Americans, Myrdal's association with Sweden made that country a role model for social progress, a role it took over, once and for all, from Denmark. Until then, a number of factors had accounted for the perception of Denmark as progressive. Particularly important on this mental matrix was the success of the agricultural system based on the spirit of thriving together—"there are no rich and no poor." In 1922, the *National Geographic Magazine* praised Denmark as "a land of co-operation and a land whose people are very highly civilized." Another factor was the Danish folk high school, with its mix of lectures, singing, conversation, physical exercises, history, and folklore, which served as a symbol of Danish originality.

Pro-Scandinavian writers at the time refrained from making any derogatory remarks about specific "races," although authors were not completely disinclined to such categories. For example, in his 1936 book *Happy Scandinavians*, Jewish-French journalist Émile Servan-Schreiber felt the need to emphasize that the typical Swedish woman was "tall and blonde, nearly perfectly resembling American movie stars." Meanwhile, in his 1935 *The Keys to Sweden*, which was published only in French but which ran through multiple editions, journalist Serge de Chessin wrote: "[The] true Nordics have not hesitated to take the Jews, persecuted in the name of the Aryan race, under their protection." Because of its social democracy, Sweden was often a target of German propaganda. De Chassin clearly struggled with the racial stereotypes of his day and sought to negotiate his situation with idiosyncratic irony: "The people of the North—the real ones—have too much respect for civil rights and intellectual values to place their blond heads beneath Hitler's cudgel. They prefer the criterion of reason to the criterion of blood purity. They contrast the Germany of Mr. Hitler with the land of Kant, who—what a scandal—was also just a vulgar short skull." The distinction between "long skulls" and "short skulls" was first made by the Swedish scholar Andreas Retzius, who began to measure human crania around 1845. He characterized Scandinavians, Germans, English, and French as "long skulls" and attributed to them "superior intellectual characteristics."

The circumstances of the time caused writers to lay their praise for Scandinavia on a bit too thick. Foreign observers elevated the region into a veritable anti-fascist bulwark. It would have disrupted the picture to admit that there were also racism and far-right movements in these idealized societies. In his 1939 book *Enlighteners of the North*, French author Louis-Charles Royer, who was determined to identify the secret to the Scandinavian countries, ultimately put the success of these societies down to providence. Royer rephrased Voltaire's famous statement "Today the light appears to us from the North" into a question: "What today from the North could bring us light?"

Before the
Second World War

Nazi propaganda—for example, Adrian Mohr's 1936 *Norway Relates Primeval History*—continued to glorify the North. Mohr's book was intended to whip up enthusiasm for Germany's state-subsidized "Strength through Joy" holiday program. It offered up another variation on the salutory effects of the northern climate: "Romantic peoples and Orientals, worn down by heat during the day, come to life when it's night. The 'Italian night'—the humidity of tropical evenings—is the soil nourishing their soul. They get enjoyment via their ears and palate. Their skin feels comfortable in silk garments. They are people of the skin, bodily people. But that race that was lured to the North consists of people of the eye. They sought out the light, not the night. The gateway to their soul was the eye, that sensory organ which takes in spatial expanses. To see, not to sit around! To look inquisitively, not to rest in tranquility! Their ever-searching soul discovered the sublimity landscapes can possess.

They were the first race of humankind that enthusiastically sought out 'viewing points.'"

Mohr interpreted the castles built by the Normans atop the cliffs of Sicily and Calabria as proof positive of his theory. Only there, he argued, was it possible for the Normans to survey things from "superior heights," as was part of their nature. He contrasted the "Germanic drive to roam" with the "Lapps," who had supposedly only followed their semidomesticated reindeer to the Arctic Ocean to "escape the terrible summer mosquito plague." Mohr came up with all sorts of connections between Norwegian and German culture. Viking ships were "examples of the oldest, purely Germanic culture" and owed their existence to "a brilliance that was exclusively Germanic." Nor did he neglect the elegantly simple stave churches, whose exclusive use of wood as a material demonstrated a deep affinity with the forest-dwelling Germanic tribes. For Mohr, "the true, thick, opulent Norwegian forest" was no different from the German variety: "In Germanic tales, the forest is full of life, not just talking animals, but talking trees and all sorts of other flora. And when the trees aren't talking out loud, they make faces and move their features, communicating their thoughts, what they want and don't want. The traveler finds this talking forest in Norway!"

The German glorification of everything connected with the North was intimately connected with Germans' sense of being surrounded by enemies to the west and east. The Third Reich's northern territorial ambitions soon focused on Norway, which at the start of World War Two had declared its neutrality and which held out for two months of German aerial bombardment before being occupied. Germany had given Norwegian King Haakon VII the choice between capitulation or death. When the monarch answered "no," Hitler replied with bombs. During the German invasion, Knut Hamsun issued a call to his compatriots: "Norwegians! Throw down your arms and return home! The Germans are fighting for us all and are now shattering England's tyranny over us and all neutrals."

As of 1942, Norway's government was led by Vidkun Quisling, the chairman of the fascist Nasjonal Samling (National Collective). Quisling had met with Hitler during the 1930s and was obviously captivated by Norse mythology: He named his villa on the Oslofjord Peninsula "Gimle" after the location in the *Prose Edda* where the survivors of the Ragnarök, the world-ending battle between gods and giants, had gathered.

The occupation of Norway was crucial to the German war machine, which depended on iron ore from Kiruna and Malmberget in Sweden and needed to secure a route from Narvik to ship it to Germany. Sweden sold its ore in return for being spared the war, leaving it cut off from the West, like Switzerland, as an island in the middle of the Nazi empire. Denmark was invaded at the same time as Norway and was occupied until the end of the war.

However, Hitler's vision for Norway went far beyond the massive military defenses built on Norway's Atlantic coast. Aware that the Norwegians were more "Aryan" than the Germans, he treated them differently from the other conquered nations, but only to a certain extent. He realized that their independent spirit had to be broken to integrate them into a common National Socialist society—always with Germany in full control. "Norwegians were to be convinced rather than compelled—steered gently toward the glorious National Socialist future that they did not yet realize they wanted," as Despina Stratigakos writes in *Hitler's Northern Utopia* (2020). "The Nazis expected that postwar Norway, like the rest of Europe, would orbit around Berlin's sun, and the development of vast infrastructure systems would move resources and people between them." The frenetic building activity that Hitler undertook in Norway included high-speed autobahns, airfields, power stations, and various commercial and industrial facilities. Since religion was not held in high esteem by the Nazis, existing churches were dwarfed with massive structures adjacent to them. A new German city and cultural capital on an island outside Trondheim was intended to be built on north-south and east-west axes in a style much different from what was considered by the Nazis as the "decadent" architecture of the 1920s and 1930s. Oslo, Norway's largest city, was seen as "degenerate" and effeminate by the

Nazis, its inhabitants influenced by Americanism, alienated from their folk past.

As if this wasn't enough, the German occupiers hallucinated a profound overhaul of the physical environment: "Norway's wild landscapes would be shaped according to German ideals of beauty and order and for German consumption," writes Stratigakos. The Nazis saw themselves as "the new Vikings, conquering with military weapons and engineering skills," and imagined the fulfillment of their vast infrastructural projects as a strange homecoming: "a return to a place that had never been theirs." Norway was projected as the wing of a postwar Germanic empire that stretched beyond the Arctic Circle, a dream tourist destination, a sort of Aryan theme park under the swastika. Hitler also wanted to break the bonds with Britain, Norway's main trading partner, limit Anglo cultural influence, and prevent an invasion.

There were much darker sides to the German occupation of Norway, among them the ruthless use of slave labor, mainly of captured Russian and Serbian prisoners of war. According to estimates, over fourteen thousand died while working in Norway. Also, Norwegian Jews were deported to Poland and murdered there. Another appalling aspect of the German occupation of Norway was to urge SS men sent there to produce more offspring to increase the birth rate among "favored races"—a eugenic program that had its roots in Social Darwinist ideas from a few decades earlier. The Lebensborn (Fount of Life) organization began its work in 1935 under Heinrich Himmler (who was also among the main architects of the Holocaust) and was extended to at least eight countries under German occupation. In Norway, the program was started in 1941. In twelve maternity facilities, single Norwegian women pregnant by German officers gave birth to their children. Since everything happened in secrecy and many documents were destroyed—to safeguard the names of unmarried mothers and officers who were often already married in Germany—or only discovered much later, the Lebensborn invited a lot of mythmaking over the decades, a morbid fascination even. The women could leave their children with the organization, which cared for them in the Lebensborn homes if they requested it. However, many of the eight thousand to twelve thousand Norwegian-German

"Home, family, fatherland"—promotional poster of the
women's branch of the Nasjonal Samling (National Collective), Norway's far-right political party, published in
1943. *Propagandaplakat Nasjonal Samling "Heim ætt fedreland," artist:*
Kaare Sørum, 1943

babies were abducted, sent to Germany for adoption, and sometimes
reclaimed by their mothers later. After the end of the German occupation,
these women faced severe discrimination and were often punished as collaborators or even deported, and the children were stigmatized. It was only
in 2018 that the Norwegian government finally apologized for these actions.

Unlike with other occupied countries, Germany invested more resources in Norway than it withdrew. But in the end, the Nazis' ambitions were thwarted when, a few years into the Second World War, their resources were more urgently needed elsewhere. The German occupation of Norway ended with the capitulation of German forces in Europe in May 1945. On May 7, 1945, Hamsun would still praise Hitler as a "reformer of the highest order" in an obituary printed in Oslo's newspaper *Aftenposten*. The author was subsequently subjected to an extensive psychiatric evaluation, which found that his mental faculties were impaired. He was ultimately convicted of criminal charges for his political statements and support for the Norwegian National Socialists, but received only a fine. He issued a defiant reply in the form of *On Overgrown Paths* (1949), an *apologia* that showed that his mental faculties were in fine standing.

Nordic enthusiasts and National Socialists didn't invariably see eye to eye. At least some of the former distanced themselves from the idea that northerners were the "leading people" and more or less convincingly disputed the notion that they were anti-Semites. Günther, for instance, wrote about what he saw as the progressive side of the Nordic movement: "It will reject all this deafening lionization of what is deemed Germanic, this flirtation with Old Germanic and Old Norse words (often incorrectly used in the singular and plural and falsely conjugated and spelled), these attempts at reanimating extinct—and often misunderstood—customs from a completely different stage of civilization, these house names borrowed from the Edda and other Norse writings, all these ridiculous outgrowths of a barren romanticization of everything Germanic." But such views didn't excuse Günther of his complicity in the larger sense. He certainly helped politicize the North for the extreme right.

Although Norse myths by no means dominated Nazi ideology, their symbols were often appropriated. Himmler, ever susceptible to mystic traditions, adopted runic letters for the uniforms of the SS and was said to participate in circles that practiced occult rites in one form or another. One such form was so-called rune gymnastics, which derived meditation positions from runic letters in a combination of yoga, ethnic esotericism, and nudism. "Rune yodeling," a kind of collective humming, also invoked the supposedly mysterious magic power of runes. An initiative launched by German mystic painter Siegfried Adolf Kummer resulted in the founding of a "runic academy" in the city of Jena in 1927. It later joined with the occult Ariosophic Summer School in the town of Bärenstein.

Those who took part in such practices, however, were treading in a minefield and could be persecuted for defaming their "Aryan legacy." Lanz von Liebenfels, a former Cistercian monk and close disciple of Guido von List, assumed a new identity to conceal his mother's Jewish ancestry, claiming to have been born in Sicily, while he authored a decades-long series of pamphlets for "blonds and advocates of male rights." It was named after the Germanic goddess of spring, Ostara, and offered advice on how to sire Aryan children. Nonetheless, Liebenfels was subject to a publishing ban. Hitler, who was familiar with such pamphlets from his years in Vienna, resisted the idea of National Socialism being turned into an explicitly religious movement or sect. In *Mein Kampf* he wrote: "It is typical of such persons that they rant about ancient Teutonic heroes of the dim and distant ages, stone axes, battle spears and shields, whereas in reality they themselves are the most woeful poltroons imaginable. . . . Thus they turn tail and run when the first communist cudgel appears. Posterity will have little occasion to write a new epic about these heroic gladiators." But Hitler would never be able to fully dispel the Nordic "ghost" or "shade" he once invoked but could no longer easily control.

The Nazis now saw Günther and his "Nordic movement" as getting in the way of their main objectives. As Christopher Hutton, professor of English at the University of Hong Kong, points out, Günther had stressed in his writings that only a part of the German population conformed to the Nordic racial idea, so this view risked promoting a racial elitism within the German populace that contradicted the ideal of an egalitarian society. The Nordic Society, which had once bragged that it was the largest German organization to serve international causes, merged with the Nordic Ring in 1936 and quickly faded into obscurity. Not even the society's publication in 1938 of a weighty *Northland Primer*, a "special edition for the work of the Hitler Youth" printed in old-fashioned Gothic type and offering a partial overview of Scandinavian history and culture, was able to prevent the society's demise. While the Nazis continued to make use of the Nordic aesthetic in their iconography, by the late 1930s, Aryan ideologues were increasingly shifting their focus east, to Indian Aryans, who were seen as a people with an advanced culture. The Nazis were fascinated by the Indian caste system, in which they saw, in Alfred Rosenberg's words, "a means," albeit a previously ineffective one, "of protecting Aryan conquerors against racial bastardization."

The Eternal Longing for the Cold Apocalypse

I t has been said that J. R. R. Tolkien was told a version of the *Lays of Sigurd*, the fragmentary remains of the *Nibelungenlied*, as a child, and this awakened his interest in Norse myths. Whether that was true or not, he later began studying Old Norse, so that he could read these tales in the original, and wrote a narrative poem entitled the *Legend of Sigurd and Gudrun*, his only work not set in the fictional Middle Earth. At Oxford he took a course in Scandinavian philology, and as a lecturer at the University of Leeds he taught Icelandic studies. In 1933, he was made an honorary member of the Icelandic Literary Society. Eight years later, in a letter to his brother Michael in June 1941, he vented his anger at "the Nazi misappropriation and perversion of the 'Nordic' spirit and myth in their quest for world domination." He added: "I have spent most of my life, since I was your age, studying Germanic matters (in the general sense that includes England and Scandinavia). There is a great deal more force (and truth) than ignorant people imagine in the 'Germanic' ideal. I was much attracted by it as an undergraduate (when Hitler was, I suppose, dabbling in paint, and had not heard of it), in reaction against the 'Classics.' . . . I have in this War a burning private grudge—which would probably make me a better soldier at 49 than I was at 22: against that ruddy little ignoramus Adolf Hitler . . . Ruining, perverting, misapplying, and making for ever accursed, that noble northern spirit, a supreme contribution to Europe, which I have ever loved, and tried to present in its true light."

Norse gods play no role in Tolkien's thousand-page-plus trilogy *The Lord of the Rings*, but there are references to the Volsungs and the dragon slayer Sigurd. There seem to be parallels with Wagner's *Ring Cycle*, and some literary scholars have found structural and thematic similarities. Tolkien categorically rebuffed any such idea, writing, "Both rings were round, but there the resemblance ceases." In terms of their political outlooks, Tolkien and Wagner were worlds apart.

Other well-known writers felt connected to the High North and even visited there. One was the Anglo-American W. H. Auden, who traveled to Iceland for three months in 1936 together with the Irish poet Louis MacNiece. The result of their trip was the 1937 travelogue *Letters from Iceland*, which combined text and photographs into a kind of collage. Auden's detailed practical recommendations showed the depth of his knowledge of the island. Addressing readers in a familiar tone, Auden tells them what to pay attention to during their visits. Auden's Iceland is a place of great hopes and an almost surreal location where connections between human beings, nature, and mythology are lively and open to observation by attentive visitors. It was also a site where Auden could liberate himself from all the impurities of modern civilization. "Europe is absent," he wrote. "This is an island and therefore unreal." Auden's picture of Iceland is idealized. Dreams suffused with myths often emerge in the forefront, and much of what the author wrote recalls the Romantic poets. Auden was convinced that he himself came from Iceland. Not only was he blond and light skinned, he also believed his last name derived from Auðunn, or Odin. What's more, Auden had also read Ida Pfeiffer's journal, and a quote of her reappears in his work: "I heard a voice in the farm singing an Icelandic song. At a distance it resembled the humming of bees."

Various factors made many Americans and Europeans long to visit Iceland. Although it was only a few hours away by plane from both North America and Europe, the idea stubbornly persisted that Iceland was another world entirely. Icelanders, it was often written, lived in a different age as though frozen in time—an impression reinforced by the island's breathtaking geological phenomena. Ironically, seen geographically, Iceland is a young island, having only existed for a scant twenty million years. The typical visit to Iceland followed the classic voyages to the High North or other putatively "untouched" regions: from civilization to the wild. Visitors encountered an unfamiliar language and were forced to rely on themselves alone.

Austrian author Christiane Ritter was a different case entirely. In 1934, she followed her husband, a ship's officer, to northern Svalbard, where she spent a whole year with him in a small hut. He had written to her: "I hope you're going to keep your promise and come up here this year. . . . It won't be too lonely for you, because at the north-east corner of the coast, about sixty miles from here, there is another hunter living, an old Swede. We can visit him in the spring, when it's light again and the sea and fiords are frozen over. . . . P.S. If you still have room in your rucksack, bring enough toothpaste for two people for a year, and also sewing needles." The book Ritter wrote about her experiences, *A Woman in the Polar Night* (published in German in 1938 and in English in 1954), was reprinted numerous times. On the jacket to the German edition, she invoked "the force of universal calm, the infinite space, the rush of the seas that passes through me and what used to be my own individual will be blown against the implacable cliffs and scattered like a little cloud." Ritter's book focused on the foreign environment of the island and the effect it had on her own personal development. One of the few diversions was her daily "walk": "It is scarcely a walk any more, rather a daily crawl on all fours close to the walls of the hut. Round and round mechanically, in circles, ten times, twenty times, over the uneven snow drifts that have frozen hard as steel. I know every inch of it, and go with my eyes closed. At first I was uncertain in the darkness. Often I would suddenly imagine a bear in front of me, but now I have found a way of dealing with my fear. At regular intervals I beat on the walls of the hut with my fist, so that the noise will scare away anything that may be in the neighborhood." For Ritter, the North was an arena for experiencing herself under extreme conditions, a personal trial by fire.

Such experiences were necessarily connected with conditions of nature, as shown by the case of British actress Constance Malleson, who traveled Norway, Sweden, and Finland from 1936 to 1946 and described her experiences in her autobiography *In the North*. Motivated by an abiding love of the North, she took in nature with all her senses and often withdrew to remote areas. To her, Finnish saunas were "an apotheosis of all experience: Purgatory and paradise; earth and fire; fire and water; sin and forgiveness. A lyrical ecstasy. It is resurrection from the dead. It is eternal new birth. It is, perhaps, a kind of symbol of the Finnish spirit. It is the most perfect communion between man and nature that the world has yet discovered."

Nonetheless, Malleson never found peace. Again and again, she was disturbed by the political conflicts of the age. In moments of desperation, she drew strength from reading the *Kalevala*, that masterpiece of Finnish epic poetry. Malleson's autobiography alternates between descriptions of dramatic events and the most precise sort of observations on nature: "Summer had come—a crescendo of berries. First, the little pine-scented, wild strawberries—everywhere in the grass and amongst the bracken fringing of the forest; more fragrant by far than the fraises des bois of Paris restaurants. Then, the whortleberries, misted with bloom like grapes; turning all the country children into juice-stained, grinning little devils. Then, the wild raspberries. And before they are gone, the earth is scattered with round ruby cranberries. Upon the market stalls, golden cloudberries appear. And up around Kuopio and further north, the delicious arctic bramble, mesimarja (*Rubus arcticus*): it has one single tiny mauve flower upon a slender stem. The berry is very like a dark raspberry—and makes a rather sweet liqueur."

Once in 1941, she suddenly found herself surrounded by German soldiers fighting the Red Army in Finland. To escape this situation, she had to row 25 miles back to Helsinki, where she succeeded in getting to Stockholm on a Swedish warship. Ultimately, she had no choice but return, heavyhearted, to her British homeland.

The Bible Is
Right After All

The end of National Socialism did not entirely spell the end of the ideology that emerged in Germany as the Nordic mythos went sour. After the war, Günther spent three years in internment and allegedly toyed with the idea of leaving the country. He decided to remain in Germany, however, where his financial situation was more secure. Working under the pseudonyms Ludwig Winter and Heinrich Ackermann, he was able to keep publishing into the 1960s. By shifting his focus to questions of heredity and mostly avoiding race as a topic, he spared himself further repercussions. But old mental habits die hard. More than a decade after the end of the Second World War, "Ludwig Winter" complained about a supposed "disappearance of Nordic blood," citing it as a major reason for the "decline of the West." Meanwhile, "Heinrich Ackermann" heaped praise on Indians for having "still retained so much of the inwardness of original, pre-Christian

Indo-Germanness . . . in contrast to the peoples and masses of Europe and North America."

In postwar Germany's social discourse, the equality of all ethnic groups was now a sine qua non and the term *race* no longer opportune. In 1951, conservative military historian Walther Hubatsch felt called to provide a sober reassessment of Germany's past obsessions in his book *The Germans and the North*. Hubatsch considered Günther to have "distanced himself from his Teutonic infatuation with all things Germanic" and portrayed his intellectual efforts as more or less innocent. However, this judgment was severely premature. At the time, Hubatsch could not know that the American Society of Human Genetics would appoint Günther as a corresponding member in 1953 or that he would continue working toward the goals he had espoused during the Nazi era with the Northern League, a conference of pan-Nordicists that was founded in 1957 in Britain. The Northern League issued a monthly publication called *The Northlander* and later transferred its headquarters to Amsterdam, with branches in Minneapolis and Capetown. The league asserted that northern Europeans represented the "purest survival of the great Indo-European family of nations, sometimes described as the Caucasian race and at other times as the Aryan race."

The anti-ideological atmosphere of postwar West Germany, however, was somewhat more receptive to other voices. One belonged to Herbert Kühn, a pioneering expert in Ice Age art. Because his wife was Jewish, the National Socialists had barred him from holding a teaching post, and he worked during the Third Reich as an independent scholar. In 1956, he wrote that it seemed "simply absurd . . . to speak of culture spreading from the North to the South; in fact, the old concept 'ex oriente lux' as laid out in the oldest book of human memory, the Bible, has been thoroughly proven true." Kühn not only taught prehistoric art in Berkeley and Detroit, but also served on the staff of New York's Museum of Modern Art.

In the mid-1950s, a German named Werner Keller landed an international best seller with a book called *The Bible as History*. In it, he argued that European culture was a legacy of influence from the ancient

Orient. Keller's book played an important role in discrediting abstruse theories that humanity, Europeans, or even northern Europeans had come from the High North, ideas that were relegated to the lunatic fringe. Keller was a departmental director in Albert Speer's Ministry of Armaments during the Third Reich, but he was also an active member of the anti-Hitler resistance who rescued Jews from the Holocaust. He only barely escaped with his own life at the end of the Second World War after the notoriously political and draconian People's Court of Nazi Germany sentenced him to death by hanging.

Despite this sea change in German attitudes, Klaus von See warned in 1970 that although "the historical constellation has changed from the ground up, and Germanic ideology and Aryan-Nordic racial mythology have disappeared from view—the components of self-conception that developed from them . . . largely remain under the surface." The recent twenty-first-century revival in Germany of the far right shows that two generations after von See's warning, such ideas continue to proliferate.

The True North

Today, the mythical North remains very much in currency. The slogan "Nordic by Nature," used, among other things, as the title of a book about Scandinavian cuisine and music, suggests that there is something unspoiled and primeval about the region—even as it echoes the name of a late-twentieth-century US rap group. The popular winter apparel and outdoor equipment brand The North Face lays implicit claim that its products can withstand the extreme climatic challenges of the uppermost north. The name refers to the north face of the Half Dome in Yosemite National Park, which is known for its difficulty as a rock climbing route, but also for being cast in shadow and more prone to frost and lingering ice. But where is the North, the oft-invoked "true North," today? Ultima Thule has been moved to outer space. In 2019, NASA gave that name to an unusual binary object in the Kuiper Belt about 4 billion miles from Earth—before critics pointed out its dubious past and the space agency renamed it Arrokoth, the Algonquin and Powhatan word for "heaven."

Our fascination with the history of northern exploration and the terrors it entailed continued to inform contemporary culture. One common trope is the retelling of real-life nineteenth-century polar expeditions fictionalized to appeal to current readers' tastes. For instance, in American author Andrea Barrett's 1998 novel *The Voyage of the Narwhal*, a fictional group of adventurers sets off to find Franklin's lost expedition. The hero, Erasmus Darwin, goes on the voyage to study Arctic flora and fauna, but the ship, the *Narwhal*, gets frozen in ice, forcing the passengers to spend the winter in the icy North. Eventually, they encounter Inuit who show them the remnants of the lost Franklin expedition.

While traditionally most explorers of the North, especially prior to the nineteenth century, were men, recently more and more women writers and researchers have ventured there. Among them is British travel writer Sara Wheeler. In *The Magnetic North: Notes from the Arctic Circle* (2009), she documents her quest to discover the meaning of "Arctic," ranging from the minute details to the larger issues like the conditions of the Chukchi in northeastern Russia, "the most brutally dispossessed of circumpolar peoples."

Environmental historian Bathsheba Demuth, in *Floating Coast* (2019), offers a groundbreaking study of the previous two centuries of material exchanges that have impacted the peoples and animals of the Bering Strait, that complex ecosystem between northeastern Russia and northwestern America, the Arctic and the Pacific Ocean. Focusing on the flow of energy from one form to another, what she calls a "chain of conversions," Demuth shows how natural resources and political-economical systems are inextricably linked. "We all live in more than one time, even if we are taught to refuse the idea," she writes.

British travel writer Kari Herbert's book *Polar Wives* (2020) profiles a cast of women behind some famous Arctic and Antarctic explorers, among them Jane Franklin, Josephine Peary, and Eva Nansen. Herbert elucidates the important role these women, formerly relegated to footnotes, played in the success of their husbands' endeavors.

This is by no means a complete enumeration of more recent work on various aspects of the North, but it would be remiss not to mention British writer Colin Thubron, who raised awareness of the vast region between Mongolia and the Arctic and the drive for identity among the Yakut people—"the iron men of Russia's north" and "a people driven in czarist times from an ancient paganism to a superficial Christianity, then converted to evangelical Communism, then stranded in wilderness." For his book *In Siberia* (2009), Thubron traveled the region at a time before record-breaking heat waves, thawing permafrost, and raging wildfires there started to make headlines.

The British novelist and essayist Joanna Kavenna's book *The Ice Museum* (2005) is another example of the imaginative attraction that the North has retained for writers up to the present. Kavenna set out for a long trip across northern Europe to search for the lost, mythic land of Thule, an activity she compares to "rebuilding an ancient temple from a few scattered stones." She sums the complication: "The uncertain provenance of Thule meant that the word could be used by anyone who found it. It could be tied to any cause, any deranged perspective on the history of the north."

When today's Norwegian explorers head off to nature, they don't always do so in their own native land. In North America, they retrace the footsteps of Helge Ingstad, who made numerous hunting trips to northern Canada and Alaska, which he documented in his 1933 book *The Land of Feast and Famine*. His depiction of how he fearlessly survived on his own through four years of trying conditions inspired whole generations of real and would-be adventurers. He also inscribed himself on the map. Ingstad Creek is the name of a small river in northwestern Canada, and Ingstad Mountain is part of the Brooks Range, the highest mountain range in the Arctic Circle. The peak was given this name after lobbying from the Nunamiut people, of whom Ingstad made copious video and audio recordings, preserving their culture, when he visited them in 1950. Ingstad also played a minor role in the history of Norwegian colonialism: In 1931, when Norway occupied an unsettled part of western Greenland, calling it Erik-the-Red and Fritjof-Nansen-Land, Ingstad was named governor. But two years later the

International Court of Justice awarded this territory to Denmark, and Norway withdrew from Greenland. Less widely known is the United States' occupation of Greenland from 1941 to the end of the Second World War to preempt a German invasion.

Ingstad was a romantic who depicted the North American North as far more pristine than it actually was. The colonialization of the region's Indigenous people—by the Americans, Russians, and Europeans, who, starting in the mid-eighteenth century, began plundering the region's resources, seeking whale oil to fuel their lamps, baleen for their wives' corsets, ivory from walrus tusks, then gold and oil—was already well underway by the time Ingstad visited them. White settlers were already working with and exploiting the Indigenous population, with women from First Nations especially being treated brutally, like slaves. The population of beaver that they hunted for their pelts had been decimated by the early twentieth century. It was only with the advent of beaver farms that the creatures living in the wild began to be spared somewhat. Agnes Deans Cameron's previously mentioned account *The New North* mentions that "the highest price for a silver-pelt ever paid on the London market" was $1,700 and "that it was one of the most beautiful skins seen in the history of the trade, and that it went to the Paris Exposition," but it is not known how much was paid to the trapper. It was a huge business, and the European market in particular was insatiable: "Of the American silver-fox . . . black skins have a ready market at from $1500 to $4000. They are used for Court robes and by the nobles."

Whatever natural resources the physical North has offered or might still offer for exploitation, the imaginary North provides a nearly inexhaustible reservoir of heroes, dramas, and adventure stories. Popular fascination with the Vikings has continued unabated. Remains (or reconstructions) of Viking ships—for example, the 122-foot-long Roskilde 6, discovered in 1997—are attractions that fire the imagination around the world. Scandinavians, of course, play an active role in keeping the mythic North alive. The Icelandic town of Hafnarfjörður, for instance, is known for its festival staging of allegedly authentic Viking life. Not without a sense of irony and humor, Icelandic businesspeople frequently invoke the customs of their forefathers and their own "inner Viking" at traditional banquets, where guests don Viking helmets and dine on putrefied shark meat (called hákarl). In this way, clichés about the North in general and Iceland in particular are simultaneously ironized and reinforced.

A 1928 English translation of an excerpt from the *Poetic Edda* reads:

For good is not, though good it is thought
mead for the sons of men;
the deeper he drinks the dimmer grows
the mind of many a man.
Drunk I became, dead drunk, forsooth
in the hall of hoary Fjalar;
that bout is best from which back fetches
each man his mind full clear.

The notion that the climate of the North encourages excessive alcohol consumption remains quite common. Observers as far back as Tacitus remarked that the Germanic tribes had a weakness for drink. And the drunken northlander remains a popular trope to this day, for instance in the popular film comedy *101 Reykjavík* by Hallgrímur Helgason (2000). It is often invoked together with unflattering clichés about the food of northern countries. Yet, Iceland had a temperance movement, and in the early twentieth century, alcohol was completely prohibited, a ban that was only gradually relaxed over the course of decades. While wine was legalized in 1922 and other alcoholic beverages in 1935, the sale of beer with an alcohol content of more than 2.25 percent remained forbidden until 1989, and the state still strictly regulates the sale of all alcohol. In Sweden, Norway, and Finland, wine and spirits can only be purchased from the shops operated by the respective state liquor monopolies, although beer or low-alcohol beer can be bought in retail grocery stores. It is beyond dispute that intoxication is part of special celebrations in the North, but that is also the case for many countries elsewhere.

A 2018 self-help book written by Chris Shern and Henrik Jeberg, published in English in Denmark and entitled *Return of the Vikings,* promises to teach the skills of "Nordic Leadership in Times of Extreme Change," drawing on "the rich legacy" and "deep roots" of the Vikings. In his most recent book, *The Viking Heart: How Scandinavians Conquered the World* (2021), conservative historian Arthur Herman sets out to explain how the Vikings supposedly shaped Europe and beyond. And not surprisingly, the Norwegian tourist association continues to this day to promote the country by invoking its Viking legacy.

Former president Donald Trump made headlines in early 2018 when he articulated preference for Norwegians over other non-Nordic and especially non-White peoples. Talking at an official Oval Office meeting about which sort of immigrants the United States should receive, he voiced his contempt for migrants from "shithole countries" in the Carribean, Africa, and South America, remarking, "We should have more people from places like Norway." Norwegians weren't particularly amused and rejected his offer. "On behalf of Norway: Thanks, but no thanks," tweeted Norwegian Conservative Party representative Torbjørn Sætre. Trump also praised Finland for assiduously raking its forests as a way of blasting California for having the temerity to be hit by massive wildfires. On the other hand, he criticized Sweden for what he thought were its high crime rates, allegedly after watching a fictional Swedish crime series on TV. But in that instance, too, he blamed the problem solely on immigrants.

Northern tales of yore remain in high demand. The immense success of the television series *Game of Thrones* (2011–2019), shot in part in Iceland, speaks for itself. US writer Neil Gaiman, the author of *American Gods,* once proposed: "The Norse myths are the myths of a chilly place, with long, long winter nights and endless summer days, myths of a people who did not entirely trust or even like their gods, although they respected and feared them." Gaiman's work attempts to transport readers back to the past, retelling myths in a form comprehensible to today's audiences. Gaiman freely admits that there are holes in our knowledge and that much has been lost. He is also well aware that the sagas and *Edda* were first written down long after Christianity had supplanted the worship of Norse dei-

Some of the tattoos displayed by this man storming the US Capitol—the valknut, the yggdrasil (the world tree), and Thor's hammer—relate to Norse mythology. His horned hat reflects the common Viking cliché. *Photo by Selcuk Acar/ NurPhoto via Getty Images*

ties. *American Gods* was inspired by a visit to Iceland. But what needs are serviced by such tales from a world that no longer exists and perhaps never did in the form that we imagine?

There can be no final verdict on the Vikings. As Jóhanna Katrín Friðriksdóttir points out in *Valkyrie: The Women of the Viking World* (2020): "We exoticize them, but upon closer examination, it emerges that we have surprisingly many things in common with the Vikings: like them, we are also living in a time of shifting gender roles, migration, fluctuating economies, new media and technology, and the global flow of goods—a time in which the world changes rapidly and unpredictably. Although we live dramatically different lifestyles, many of the more existential concerns with which we are preoccupied would have been familiar to a Norse person."

Many contemporary Americans still identify deeply with Scandinavia—this is particularly true in North Dakota, Minnesota, Wisconsin, Iowa, and northern Illinois. In his 2014 book *Vikings in the Attic: In Search of Nordic America*, Eric Dregni writes: "Many Midwesterners refer to themselves as simply 'Norwegian' or 'Finnish,' not 'Norwegian American' or 'Finnish American,' even though many have never been to Scandinavia and can't speak the language. Most are third-, fourth-, or even fifth-generation Scandinavians who can claim whichever of their many different backgrounds they want to be." There have been state-supported efforts in Minnesota to rebrand the state as "the North" rather than "the Midwest."

How does the current affinity for the North compare with the sentimental mindset of the eighteenth- and nineteenth-century Romantics? There are no coastlines or mountains anymore that haven't been measured, nor any Arctic waters that don't bear traces of contamination from human civilization—plastics in the ocean or acid rain and radiation in the farthest reaches of the North. Travelers to the High North are looking for stillness and long to withdraw from civilization into sparsely settled landscapes and barely altered nature. They aren't afraid of the darkness in winter.

Canada, along with the United States (Alaska), Russia, Denmark (including Greenland and the Faroe Islands), Iceland, Sweden, and Finland, is one of the circumpolar nations of the world, and it has certainly come a long way since the legendary 1922 film *Nanook of the North* in recognizing how central its northern regions are to its national and cultural identity. It's difficult to gauge how much this discussion or negotiation of identity is known beyond Canada, but artists and thinkers have engaged it in a variety of genres. Pianist Glenn Gould's cryptic sound documentary *The Idea of North* (1967) layered speaking voices from interviews on top of each other, where every interviewee offered contrasting views of northern

Canada. As Gould explained in his introduction: "I've been intrigued for a long time . . . by the incredible tapestry of tundra and taiga country. . . . I've read about it, written about it occasionally, and even pulled up my parka once and gone there. But like all but a very few Canadians, I guess, I've had no direct confrontation with the northern third of our country. I've remained of necessity an outsider, and the North has remained for me a convenient place to dream about, spin tall tales about sometimes, and, in the end, avoid."

For Margaret Atwood, "the North focuses our anxieties. Turning to face north, face the north, we enter our own unconscious. Always, in retrospect, the journey north has the quality of dream." At the same time the Canadian North is an inexhaustible source of artistic inspiration, it's also a battleground for concrete economic and political interests. In 1999, Nunavut—the newest, northernmost, and largest territory—was declared to belong to the Inuit population and their independent government. Ten years before, Canadian writer Rudy Wiebe included an upside-down map of the North in his collection of essays *Playing Dead: A Contemplation Concerning the Arctic*, offering an Inuit view of the South.

Canadian geographer Louis-Edmond Hamelin, in the early 1960s, coined the term *nordicité*, coming up with a list of criteria, with the maximum value being reached at the geographical North Pole. Hamelin distinguished between the Extreme North, Far North, Middle North, and Near North and concluded that demographic and economic shifts, together with climate change, had led to a "denorthernization." The attempt to get a clear grip on what represents the North may be appealing, but Hamelin's theory is simply too inflexible. The North isn't something that has existed forever in a specific form. It's perennially been subject to historical transformation, forever reinvented and reconstructed.

The unspoiled world of painter Carl Larsson, Selma Lagerlöf's story of *Nils Holgersson* (1906/07), and Astrid Lindgren's *Pippi Longstockings* (1945), the strongest girl in the world—there is a continuity between these romantic images of the North from earlier decades and those of today. Older vintage Ikea catalogs recall Larsson's soft-focus idylls, if in less jingoistic

fashion, with their "typically Swedish" affinity with nature, love of children, liberalism, and sense of environmental responsibility. Not surprisingly, a country whose population more or less exists in darkness for half
of the year particularly cherishes light and brightness. One can trace early
sources for the light and airy aesthetic of Ikea furniture and decor to the
times of Swedish king Gustav III in the eighteenth century. The "Gustavian
style," a variant of French classicism, featured rather muted color palettes
and made use of native woods such as birch, beech, and pine. Later, this
developed into the less formal Swedish country style and further paved the
way for the "Scandinavian design" of today.

Scandinavian countries continue to be identified with the social welfare
state, progress, and the future, which makes many people long to travel
north. The Danish concept of *hygge*—of being cozy inside at home—has
become a lifestyle phenomenon in many countries. This general sense
of well-being has no need for romanticized and often false images of the
rural life of yesteryear. It is a product of the candlelit here and now. More
recently, during the coronavirus pandemic, the Norwegian idea of *frilufts-
liv*, of spending lots of time outdoors and cultivating a close bond with
nature, has attracted media attention worldwide. And the fame and popularity of Greta Thunberg have reinforced Scandinavia's image as being
nature loving and environmentally aware, if in a new, unfamiliar, politically active form with millions of supporters worldwide.

Northern European traditions and theses from the *Edda* and the sagas
are reaffirmed in the present across popular media. American comics like
The Mighty Thor and Japanese manga translate Old Norse stories, or at least
what the authors think are Old Norse stories, into visual terms. Computer
games do the same. Moreover, countless hard rock and heavy metal bands
have drawn inspiration from the Icelandic past. They encompass everyone
from Led Zeppelin (most prominently "Immigrant Song") to rather more
obscure acts like Solarsteinn (from Italy), Týr (from the Faroe Islands), and
the Mexican band Mighty Thor.

These comparatively harmless examples of an idealization of the
North should not blind us to less innocent phenomena associated with

the continuing popularity of Old Norse tales and Scandinavian deities. A contemporary Germanic paganism, called Ásatrú, has been attracting followers for decades, spawning communities in Canada, the United States, Britain, Scandinavia, Germany, and Australia. Its believers worship Odin. The movement heroicizes northern European pre-Christian traditions and preaches the alleged superiority of the White race. Images of Valhalla, the imaginary heaven reserved for Viking warriors, often inform this ideology together with fears that Europe is a spiritual homeland under threat by immigration from Muslim countries and condemned to destruction. Racist, anti-Muslim, and anti-immigrant sentiments are rife among such groups, which have repeatedly clashed with the law. Haithabu (from the Old Norse term *Heiðabýr*, from *heiðr*, "heathen," and *býr*, "yard") is an important archaeological museum built at the site of a former Viking trading post for herring, grain, and cloth near the North German city of Schleswig. It illustrates the lifeways of the early Middle Ages. It has also become a pilgrimage destination for neo-Nazis. Likewise, the Middle Age Viking festival held annually at the site of a former Viking settlement in the Polish town of Wolin, in the Baltic, attracts right-wing visitors from Germany and Russia who bear shields and wear T-shirts and tattoos sporting swastikas, SS skulls, and the slogan "blood and honor," as if these correspond with the historic reality of the Vikings.

Since the mid-1960s, Marxist authors and former journalists Maj Sjöwall and Per Walhöö have inaugurated a golden age of Scandinavian crime fiction—earlier in his career, Walhöö translated the police novels of the American Ed McBain into Swedish. Sjöwall and Walhöö succeeded in getting their readers interested in social criticism and politics—readers who were otherwise just looking for entertainment. Following in their footsteps were genre-bending authors like Henning Mankell, Håkan Nesser, Karin Fossum, and Stieg Larsson. In the context of this book, the Norwegian Jo Nesbø's novel *The Redbreast* (2000) is particularly worth mentioning, since the protagonist, a man intent on killing the Norwegian crown prince, is a former Nazi collaborator who, at the end of his life, wants to take revenge. Their books often leave readers wondering how much the crime and brutality described corresponds with contemporary Scandinavian social reality. Statistics show that, on average, the crime rate there isn't particularly high, although gang violence and killings in Malmö and Stockholm have put Sweden in the news recently. The monstrous 2011 terrorist attack by the Norwegian right-wing radical Anders Breivik, who killed seventy-seven people at a summer camp on the island of Utøya, shocked the world and highlighted the problem of a small but extremely violent Scandinavian racist fringe. Breivik has claimed that he sees himself as an heir to Madison Grant.

Foreign observers are sometimes dumbfounded by the strong sense of national identity Scandinavians maintain to this day. Many Norwegians, for example, are intensely proud of Viking history and the heroism of the Norwegian kings, dress up in traditional rural garb when the occasion calls for it, and see no problem with the fact that such attitudes and behavior don't fit in with conventional political distinctions between the left and right.

Last Diamonds

In 1949, when Ernst Herrmann, the northern explorer and second-in-charge of the 1938–1939 German Antarctic Expedition, published his book *The North Polar Sea: The Mediterranean of Tomorrow*, he didn't suspect the strategical importance the High North would accrue in the future. Although climate change and global warming had been measured for several years prior to his book, Herrmann wrote that "increased cooling will have to be reckoned with for the coming decades." Herrmann was a passionate advocate of "the possibility of trans-Arctic travel," arguing that humanity could no long afford "to leave whole regions of the earth unused simply for emotional reasons."

Herrmann was wrong about the planet cooling off, but he was right about nearly everything else. As the polar ice recedes more and more, the Northeast Passage will become fully navigable in the foreseeable future—it's already possible between July and October. In many cases, this will allow goods to be transported a third more quickly from Northeast Asia to western Europe than via the Suez or Panama Canal. In a few decades, scientists estimate, Arctic ships will no longer need ice-breaking hulls. Shipping traffic will bring problems previously unknown to the Arctic: noise pollution, invasive plant and animal species and oil slicks that will further damage the region's delicate ecological balance. What's more, drilling for oil in the High North will have massive consequences for its still largely untouched landscapes.

Italian artist Francesco Bosso has traveled to Greenland to photograph icebergs, arranging his images like works of art. He conceives of them as "last diamonds . . . precious jewels of nature at risk of extinction." In Bosso's strikingly dramatic black-and-white images, the gigantic blocks of ice are like fantastic reverse silhouettes battling for survival against the hostile, dark elements.

Bosso's unique iceberg photos would have undeniably deserved a spot in Ole Worm's cabinet of wonders, which has been recreated and commented on in three-dimensional form by contemporary American photographer Rosamond Wolff Purcell on the basis of Wingendorp's 1655 engraving. Originally exhibited in Santa Monica in 2003, Purcell's extraordinary work, which gives modern audiences the chance to directly experience the cabinet, found a permanent home in the geological section of the Natural History Museum of Denmark in Copenhagen.

The reconstruction prominently features the great auk, that flightless, now extinct bird that used to populate broad stretches of northern Europe, Iceland, Canada, and the eastern United States and once kept Worm company (he had received the live animal from the Faroe Islands). A couple of years ago, an international team of scientists unveiled a project to reawaken this long-gone species by extracting DNA from the remains of individual specimens, deciphering its genetic code, and injecting particularly characteristic genes into the cells of its closest living relative, the razor-billed auk. Embryos would than be transplanted to geese, which, in contrast to surviving auk species, would be large enough to give birth to a great auk. As resurrections go, this one is admittedly not particularly romantic.

The contemporary rendering of Ole Worm's chamber of wonders by Rosamond Purcell. *Natural History Museum of Denmark*

And what of the narwhal, the "northern unicorn" introduced at the beginning of this book? Barry Lopez's 1986 book *Arctic Dreams* vividly depicts these bizarre creatures, whose tusks spiral from their foreheads and who swim through the icy blue sea below floes of ice, entirely unmindful of compass points and territorial boundaries. Lopez writes that in summer, more than three-quarters of the planet's narwhal population can be found in Canada, in the Lancaster Sound north of Baffin Island, and that the word *narwhal* is possibly derived from the Old Norse *nár* and *hvalr*, meaning "corpse" and "whale." A part of the mythology surrounding these creatures included the idea that narwhals are poisonous and even fond of killing humans—which, of course, is untrue. Another theory is that *nahvalr* was the western Norwegian expression for a whale with a long canine tooth, although the most recent research indicates that such teeth are rarely found in females of the species. Lopez also writes that ship traffic in warming waters has upset the ecological balance in Arctic waters. Narwhals, as sensitive creatures, have been enormously affected, along with their main enemies, the orcas. Further warming of Arctic waters will extend the hunting grounds of the orcas and threaten the narwhals even more.

The narwhal's tusk, up to 10 feet in length, is not a useful implement for self-defense. In reality, it's just a left canine tooth that pokes through the creature's upper lip. Interestingly, it's a tooth that all male and 15 percent of female narwhals sport—which contradicts the earlier idea that it could symbolize male potency only. Narwhals can, however, use their thick skulls to batter holes through moderately thick ice in order to breathe.

When examining the North, one can refer back again and again to Worm's cabinet of wonders—whether it's the engraving or Purcell's marvelous three-dimensional, twenty-first-century reconstruction. It is a point of orientation, containing something atemporal, almost magical, that connects the centuries—where melancholy is inevitable because it reminds us of what has already gotten lost in the past and could get lost in the future as human civilization presses forward to the most remote corners of our planet.

At the same time, the human search for the *genius loci* of the North, its spirit, continues unabated. In northwestern Canada, you can board an airplane to get a look at the northern lights from an elevation of 40,000 feet. But does that get you any closer to the secrets of the North?

Acknowledgments

This book goes back to the German edition. I'm very grateful to Wolfgang Hörner, the editor of Galiani Berlin, who helped come up with the idea for this book. My gratitude goes out to Olivia Kuderewski, Detlef Feussner, Jette Anders, Tobias Becker, and Stephan Michael Schröder for reading through early versions of the manuscript and making many helpful suggestions. The friendly staff of the Staatsbibliothek in Berlin and of the Scandinavian Studies Branch Library at Humboldt University of Berlin were of great help.

I was very lucky that Alane Salierno Mason, vice president and executive editor at W. W. Norton, took an interest in this book. I am also happy that Jefferson Chase agreed to render it into English, building on some chapters that had been translated by Lori Lantz. Thanks go to Andrew Nestingen, who agreed to read the manuscript and made many useful suggestions. I would also like to thank editorial assistant Mo Crist and every-body involved in this project at W. W. Norton. The text of the German original was expanded and revised for this English edition. Also, I would like to thank Iris Brandt, rights manager of Kiepenheuer & Witsch, literary agent Cecile Barendsma and New Books in German for selecting the book, and the Goethe Institute for supporting the translation.

As a young man, I was able to travel to Scandinavia on several occa-sions. I took one of these trips with my parents, whom I would also like to thank for that experience. I made other trips as part of a group, and I embarked on a few more alone or with friends. My intensive courses in Swedish from Helena Björkman at the time were also very helpful. Without the unforgettable images I saw and my indelible memories of the marvel-ous landscapes and people I encountered, also during more recent trips to Scandinavia, I would surely have never written this book.

Any mistakes in this book are my own.

Selected Bibliography

Andrews, Malcolm. *The Search for the Picturesque: Landscape Aesthetics and Tourism in Britain 1760–1800*. Stanford: Stanford University Press, 1989.

Auden, W. H., and Louis MacNeice. *Letters from Iceland*. London: Faber & Faber, 2002.

Barraclough, Eleanor, Danielle Marie Cudmore, and Stefan Donecker, eds. *Imagining the Supernatural North*. Edmonton, Canada: Polyna Press, 2016.

Barton, H. Arnold. *Northern Arcadia. Foreign Travelers in Scandinavia, 1765–1815*. Carbondale and Edwardsville: Southern Illinois University Press, 1998.

Beamish, North Ludlow, and Carl Christian Rafn. *The Discovery of America by the Northmen in the Tenth Century*. London: T. and W. Boone, 1841.

Bellemaire-Page, Stephanie, Daniel Chartier, Alice Duhan, and Maria Walecka-Garbalinska, eds. *Le lieu du Nord: Vers une cartographie des lieux du Nord*. Quebec: University of Quebec Press, 2015.

Bohrer, Karl Heinz. "*Der Mythos vom Norden. Studien zur romantischen Geschichtsprophetie*." Unpublished dissertation, Cologne, 1961.

Böldl, Klaus. *Götter und Mythen des Nordens: Ein Handbuch*. Munich: C. H. Beck, 2013.

Böldl, Klaus, and Andreas Vollmer, eds. *Isländersagas. Texte und Kontexte.* Frankfurt: Fischer, 2011.

Boym, Svetlana. *The Future of Nostalgia.* New York: Basic Books, 2001.

Brodsky, Joseph. *Less Than One: Selected Essays.* London: Penguin, 2011.

Byrne, Angela. *Geographies of the Romantic North. Science, Antiquarianism, and Travel, 1790–1830.* New York: Palgrave Macmillan, 2013.

Campbell, Nancy. *Fifty Words for Snow.* London: Elliott & Thompson, 2020.

Chartier, Daniel. "Towards a Grammar of the Idea of North: Nordicity, Winterity." *Nordlit,* no. 22, 2007.

Chartier, Daniel. *Le lieu du Nord: Vers une cartographie des lieux du Nord.* Quebec: University of Quebec Press, 2015.

Davidson, Peter. *The Idea of North.* London: Reaktion Books, 2005.

Demuth, Bathsheba. *Floating Coast: An Environmental History of the Bering Strait.* New York: W. W. Norton, 2019.

Diamond, Jared. *Collapse: How Societies Choose to Fail or Suceed.* New York: Viking, 2005.

Dregni, Eric. *Vikings in the Attic: In Search of Nordic America.* Minneapolis: University of Minnesota Press, 2014.

Duffy, Cian, ed. *Romantic Norths: Anglo-Nordic Exchanges, 1770–1842.* London: Palgrave Macmillan, 2017.

Engel-Braunschmidt, Annelore, Gerhard Fouquet, Wiebke von Hinden, and Inken Schmidt, eds. *Ultima Thule: Bilder des Nordens von der Antike bis zur Gegenwart.* Frankfurt: Lang, 2001.

Epstein, B. J., ed. *True North: Literary Translation in the Nordic Countries.* Newcastle upon Tyne: Cambridge Scholars Publishing, 2014.

Erikson, Patricia Pierce. "Josephine Diebitsch Peary (1863–1955)." *Arctic* 62, no. 2 (March 2009): 102–104.

Felsch, Philipp. *Wie August P⁰⁺ .ann den Nordpol erfand.* Munich: Luchterhand Literaturverlag, 2010

Findell, Martin. *Runes.* London: The British Museum Press, 2014.

Fjågesund, Peter. *The Dream of the North: A Cultural History to 1920.* Amsterdam: Editions Rodopi, 2014.

Friðriksdóttir, Jóhanna Katrín. *Valkyrie: The Women of the Viking World.* London: Bloomsbury Academic, 2020.

Fülberth, Andreas, Albert Meier, and Victor Andrés, eds. *Nördlichkeit—Romantik—Erhabenheit. Apperzeptionen der Nord/Süd-Differenz (1750–2000).* Frankfurt: Lang, 2008.

Gammelien, Stefan. *Wilhelm II und Schweden-Norwegen 1888–1905. Spielräume und Grenzen eines persönlichen Regiments.* Berlin: Berliner Wissenschafts-Verlag, 2012.

Garnett, Robert R. *From Grimes to Brideshead: The Early Novels of Evelyn Waugh.* London: Associated University Presses, 1990.

Gaupseth, Silje, Marie-Theres Federhofer, and Per Pippin Aspaas, eds. *Travels in the North: A Multidisciplinary Approach to the Long History of Northern Travel Writing.* Hanover, Germany: Wehrhahn, 2013.

Godwin, Joscelyn. *Arktos: The Polar Myth in Science, Symbolism, and Nazi Survival.* Kempton, IL: Adventures Unlimited Press, 1996.

Goodrick-Clarke, Nicholas. *The Occult Roots of Nazism: Secret Aryan Cults and Their Influence on Nazi Ideology.* London: I. B. Tauris, 2004.

Grace, Sherrill. *Canada and the Idea of North.* Montreal: McGill-Queen's University Press, 2007.

Greenblatt, Stephen. *The Rise and Fall of Adam and Eve.* New York: W. W. Norton, 2017.

Haarmann, Harald. *Die Indoeuropäer.* Munich: C. H. Beck, 2010.

Hamann, Brigitte. *Die Familie Wagner.* Reinbek: Rowohlt, 2005.

Hamann, Brigitte. *Hitler's Vienna: A Dictator's Apprenticeship.* Oxford: Oxford University Press, 1999.

Hannett, Lisa L. "The Politics of Retelling of Norse Mythology." *The Atlantic,* February 23, 2017.

Hansson, Heidi, and Anka Ryall. *Arctic Modernities: The Environmental, the Exotic and the Everyday.* Newcastle upon Tyne: Cambridge Scholars Publishing, 2017.

Hatfield, Philip J. *Lines in the Ice. Exploring the Roof of the World.* Montreal: McGill-Queen's University Press, 2016.

Helgason, Jón Karl. *Echoes of Valhalla. The Afterlife of the Eddas and Sagas.* London: Reaktion Books, 2017.

Henningsen, Bernd, ed. *Begegnungen. Deutschland und der Norden im 19. Jahrhundert.* Berlin: Berlin Verlag Arno Spitz, 2000.

Henningsen, Bernd, ed. *Das Projekt Norden. Essays zur Konstruktion einer europäischen Region.* Berlin: Berlin Verlag Arno Spitz, 2002.

Herbert, Kari. *Polar Wives: The Remarkable Women behind the World's Most Daring Explorers.* Vancouver: Greystone Books, 2012.

Herman, Arthur. *The Idea of Decline in Western History.* New York: The Free Press, 1997.

Hinrichs, Nina. *Caspar David Friedrich—ein deutscher Künstler des Nordens.* Kiel, Germany: Ludwig, 2011.

Holm, Michael Juul, Mathias Ussing Seeberg, and Poul Erik Tøjner, eds. *Arctic.* Copenhagen: Louisiana Museum of Art, 2013.

Hormuth, Dennis, and Maike Schmidt, eds. *Norden und Nördlichkeit—Darstellung vom Eigenen und Fremden.* Frankfurt: Lang, 2010.

Hubatsch, Walther. *Die Deutschen und der Norden.* Göttingen, Germany: Verlag Otto Schwartz, 1951.

Hunter, Douglas. *Beardmore: The Viking Hoax That Rewrote History.* Montreal: McGill-Queen's University Press, 2018.

Hutton, Christopher. "Racial Ideology as Elite Discourse: Nordicism and the Visual in an Age of Mass Culture." *Social Semiotics* 27, no. 3 (2017).

Ibler, Gerd. *Karl Ludwig Giesecke (1761–1833). "Das Leben und Wirken eines frühen europäischen Gelehrten. Protokoll eines merkwürdigen Lebensweges."* Announcements of the Austrian Mineralogical Society 156 (2010).

Isleiffson, Sumarlidi R., ed. *Iceland and Images of the North.* Quebec: University of Quebec Press, 2011.

Jakobsson, Sverrir, ed. *Images of the North. Histories—Identities—Ideas.* Amsterdam: Rodopi, 2009.

Jennings, Andrew, Silke Reeploeg, and Angela Watt, eds. *Northern Atlantic Islands and the Sea: Seascapes and Dreamscapes.* Newcastle upon Tyne: Cambridge Scholars Publishing, 2017.

Kant, Immanuel. *Natural Science.* Cambridge, UK: Cambridge University Press, 2012.

Kavenna, Joanna. *The Ice Museum: In Search of the Lost Land of Thule.* New York: Viking, 2005.

Keller, Ulrike, ed. *Reisende im Nordmeer seit dem Jahr 530.* Vienna: Promedia, 2009.

Kent, Neil. *The Soul of the North: A Social, Architectural and Cultural History of the Nordic Countries, 1700–1940.* London: Reaktion Books, 2001.

Kinzler, Sonja, and Doris Tillmann, eds. *Nordlandreise: Die Geschichte einer touristischen Entdeckung. Historien om oppdagelsen av turistmålet Norge.* Hamburg: Mare Verlag, 2010.

Kliemann, Hendriette. *Koordinaten des Nordens. Wissenschaftliche Konstruktionen einer europäischen Region 1770–1850.* Berlin: Berliner Wissenschafts-Verlag, 2005.

Kraus, Karl. *In These Great Times: A Karl Kraus Reader.* Edited by Harry Zohn. Manchester, UK: Carcanet Press, 1984.

Krueger, David M. *Myths of the Rune Stone: Viking Martyrs and the Birthplace of America.* Minneapolis: University of Minnesota Press, 2015.

Lavin, Talia. *Culture Warloards: My Journey into the Dark Web of White Supremacy.* New York: Hachette, 2020.

Lerner, Marion. *Von der ödesten und traurigsten Gegend zur Insel der Träume. Islandreisebücher im touristischen Kontext.* Munich: Herbert Utz Verlag, 2015.

Lilienthal, Georg. *Der "Lebensborn e. V. ": Ein Instrument nationalsozialistischer Rassenpolitik.* Frankfurt: Fischer, 2003.

Lutzhöft, Hans-Jürgen. *Der Nordische Gedanke in Deutschland 1920–1940*. Stuttgart: Klett Verlag, 1971.

Lytton, Edward Bulwer. *The Novels and Romances of Edward Bulwer Lytton: Zanoni; Zicci*. Boston: Little, Brown & Company, 1897.

MacCarthy, Fiona. "William Morris in Iceland." *The Guardian*, March 26, 2010.

Manco, Jean. *Ancestral Journeys: The Peopling of Europe from the First Venturers to the Vikings*. London: Thames & Hudson, 2013.

Maner, Brent. *Germany's Ancient Pasts. Archaeology and Historical Interpretation since 1700*. Chicago: University of Chicago Press, 2018.

Marschall, Birgit. *Reisen und Regieren. Die Nordlandfahrten Kaiser Wilhelms II*. Heidelberg: Carl Winter Universitätsverlag, 1991.

Martynkewicz, Wolfgang. *Salon Deutschland. Geist und Macht 1900–1945*. Berlin: Aufbau Verlag, 2011.

Meier, Allison. "Ole Worm Returns: An Iconic 17th Century Curiosity Cabinet Is Obsessively Recreated." *Atlas Obscura*, April 30, 2013.

Mercer, Wendy S. *The Life and Travels of Xavier Marmier (1808–1892): Bringing World Literature to France*. Oxford: Oxford University Press, 2007.

Mian, Marzio G. *Artico. La battaglia per il Grande Nord*. Vicenza, Italy: Neri Pozza, 2018.

Morris, William. *The Collected Works of William Morris*. Cambridge, UK: Cambridge University Press, 2012.

Münkler, Herfried. *Die Deutschen und ihre Mythen*. Berlin: Rowohlt Berlin, 2009.

Munz-Krines, Marion. *Expeditionen ins Eis. Historische Polarreisen in der Literatur*. Frankfurt: Lang, 2009.

Musial, Kazimierz. *Roots of the Scandinavian Model. Images of Progress in the Age of Modernisation*. Baden-Baden: Nomos, 2002.

Niem, Christina. *Eugen Diederichs und die Volkskunde. Ein Verleger und seine Bedeutung für die Wissenschaftsentwicklung*. Münster: Waxmann Verlag, 2015.

Nigrisoli Wärnhjelm, Vera, and Alessandro Aresti. "*Sul Viaggio settentrionale (1700) di Francesco Negri. Con uno spoglio lessicale degli scandinavismi*." *Carte de Viaggio* 8 (2015): 43–71.

Nuttall, Mark, ed. *Encyclopedia of the Arctic*. New York: Routledge, 2005.

O'Donoghue, Heather. *From Asgard to Valhalla: The Remarkable History of the Norse Myths*. London: I. B. Tauris, 2007.

Olender, Maurice. *The Languages of Paradise: Race, Religion, and Philology in the Nineteenth Century*. Cambridge, MA: Harvard University Press, 1992.

Oslund, Karen. *Iceland Imagined: Nature, Culture, and Storytelling in the North Atlantic*. Seattle: University of Washington Press, 2011.

Ørskov, Frederik Forrai. "From Nordic Romanticism to Nordic Modernity: Danish Tourist Brochures in Nazi Germany, 1929–1939." *Journal of Contemporary History* 55 (2019): 29–51.

Patey, Douglas Lane. *The Life of Evelyn Waugh: A Critical Biography.* Oxford: Blackwell Publishers, 1998.

Piper, Ernst. *Alfred Rosenberg: Hitlers Chefideologe.* Munich: Karl Blessing Verlag, 2005.

Pöhl, Friedrich. "Assessing Franz Boas' Ethics in His Arctic and Later Anthropological Fieldwork." *Études/Inuit/Studies* 32, no. 2 (2008): 35–52.

Poliakov, Léon. *The Aryan Myth: A History of Racist and Nationalist Ideas in Europe.* New York: Basic Books, 1974.

Povlsen, Karen Klitgaard, ed. *Northbound: Travels, Encounters and Constructions 1700–1830.* Aarhus, Denmark: Aarhus University Press, 2008.

Ray, Sarah Jaquette, and Kevin Maier, eds. *Critical Norths: Space, Nature, Theory.* Fairbanks: University of Alaska Press, 2017.

Richter, Dieter. *Der Süden. Geschichte einer Himmelsrichtung.* Berlin: Verlag Klaus Wagenbach, 2009.

Robilant, Andrea di. *Venetian Navigators. The Voyage of the Zen Brothers to the Far North.* London: Faber and Faber, 2011.

Royer, Louis-Charles. *Lumières du Nord: Scènes et enseignements de la vie scandinave.* Paris: Les Éditions de France, 1939.

Rozwadowski, Helen M. *Vast Expanses: A History of the Oceans.* London: Reaktion Books, 2018.

Ryall, Anka, Johan Schimanski, and Henning Howlid Wærp, eds. *Arctic Discourses.* Newcastle upon Tyne: Cambridge Scholars Publishing, 2010.

Safranski, Rüdiger. *Romantik. Eine deutsche Affäre.* Munich: Carl Hanser Verlag, 2007.

Schepelern, H. D. *"Museum Wormianum: Dets Forutsætninger och Tilblivelse."* Dissertation with summary in English. Copenhagen, 1971.

Schlözer, August Ludwig von. *Allgemeine Nordische Geschichte.* Halle, Germany: Gebauer, 1771.

Schmidt, Wolf Gerhard. *Homer des Nordens' und, Mutter der Romantik'. James Macphersons Ossian und seine Rezeption in der deutschsprachigen Literatur.* Berlin: Walter de Gruyter, 2003.

Schnapp, Alain. *The Discovery of the Past.* New York: Abrams, 1997.

Schulz, Kathryn. "Polar Expressed: What If an Ancient Story about the Far North Came True?" *New Yorker,* April 24, 2017.

See, Klaus von. *Deutsche Germanen-Ideologie. Vom Humanismus bis zur Gegenwart.* Frankfurt: Athenäum-Verlag, 1970.

Semmens, Kristin. *Seeing Hitler's Germany: Tourism in the Third Reich.* New York: Palgrave Macmillan, 2005.

Serwer, Adam. "White Nationalism's Deep American Roots." *The Atlantic*, June 2019.

Simek, Rudolf. *Vinland! Wie die Wikinger Amerika entdeckten.* Munich: C. H. Beck, 2016.

Spiro, Jonathan Peter. *Defending the Master Race: Conservation, Eugenics, and the Legacy of Madison Grant.* Burlington: University of Vermont Press, 2009.

Spufford, Francis. *I May Be Some Time: Ice and the English Imagination.* New York: Picador, 1997.

Stratigakos, Despina. *Hitler's Northern Utopia: Building the New Order in Occupied Norway.* Princeton: Princeton University Press, 2020.

Sullivan, Paul. *Waking Up in Iceland: Sights and Sounds from Europe's Coolest Hotspot.* London: Sanctuary Publishing, 2003.

Taetz, Sascha. *Richtung Mitternacht: Wahrnehmung und Darstellung Skandinaviens in Reiseberichten städtischer Bürger des 16. und 17. Jahrhunderts.* Frankfurt: Lang, 2004.

Tallack, Malachy. *60 Degrees North. Around the World in Search of Home.* Edinburgh: Polygon, 2016.

Thubron, Colin. *In Siberia.* New York: Harper, 2000.

Truitt, E. R. "Fantasy North." *Aeon*, February 15, 2016.

Vidal-Naquet, Pierre. *The Atlantis Story: A Short History of Plato's Myth.* Liverpool: Liverpool University Press, 2007.

Watson, Peter. *The German Genius: Europe's Third Renaissance, the Second Revolution, and the Twentieth Century.* New York: Harper, 2010.

Wawn, Andrew. *The Vikings and the Victorians: Inventing the Old North in Nineteenth-Century Scandinavia.* Cambridge, UK: Brewer, 2000.

Wells, Marie. *The Discovery of Nineteenth-Century Scandinavia.* London: Norvik Press, 2008.

Wheeler, Sara. *The Magnetic North: Notes from the Arctic Circle.* New York: Farrar, Straus, and Giroux, 2011 (published by Jonathan Cape, London, in 2009 as *The Magnetic North: Travels in the Arctic*).

Wiebe, Rudy. *Playing Dead: A Contemplation Concerning the Arctic.* Edmonton: NeWest Press, 1989.

Zabel, Tobias. *Nach Schottland also! Schottlandwahrnehmungen und Deutungen deutscher Reisender zwischen Romantik und Sachlichkeit von 1800–1870.* Frankfurt: Lang, 2013.

Zahrtmann, Christian. "Remarks on the Voyages to the Northern Hemisphere Ascribed to the Zeni of Venice." *Journal of the Royal Geographic Society*, no. 5, 1835.

Index

Page numbers in *italics* refer to illustrations.